DHARMA ARTHA KAMA MOKSHA

By the same author

DHARMA
ARTHA
KAMA
MOKSHA

40 INSIGHTS INTO HAPPINESS

Devdutt Pattanaik

Illustrations by the author

Harper
Collins

First published in hardback in India by
HarperCollins *Publishers* in 2021
A-75, Sector 57, Noida, Uttar Pradesh 201301, India
www.harpercollins.co.in

2 4 6 8 10 9 7 5 3 1

Text and illustrations copyright © Devdutt Pattanaik 2021

P-ISBN: 9789354224447
E-ISBN: 9789354224454

Typeset in Garamond by Special Effects Graphics Design Co., Mumbai

Printed and bound at
Thomson Press (India) Ltd

Contents

Introduction

How can we as human beings live a happy and meaningful life (purusha-artha)?

According to ancient Hindu scriptures there are four pillars (chatur-varga) that can help us do that: dharma, artha, kama, moksha.

- Dharma is about one's responsibility to society at large.
- Artha is about achievement and success.
- Kama is about intimacy, sensual and sexual pleasures.
- Moksha is about freedom from bondage and worldly suffering.

To appreciate this concept, we need to hear the story of Indra, King of Paradise, who one day called upon his architect, Vishwakarma, to build him a palace worthy of godly glory. Vishwakarma built Indra a palace, but it didn't satisfy the king. So, he built a bigger and grander palace. But even this was not good enough for Indra, and Vishwakarma built yet another palace. But no matter what Vishwakarma created, Indra remained unsatisfied—Indra felt that his glory was not matched by the opulence of the structures Vishwakarma was building. Desperate, Vishwakarma went to Vishnu and asked for help. Vishnu appeared in front of Indra, in the form of a child. Indra took him around, showing him the many palaces built by Vishwakarma. Indra then very sheepishly added that none of them really matched his greatness. Vishnu, as the little boy, was not impressed and informed Indra that, although wonderful, his palaces were not as wonderful as the palaces of all the Indras who had lived before him.

This comment startled Indra, and he asked the boy what he meant by 'lived before him': wasn't he unique? The boy laughed and replied that there were many Indras in the world: there had been many Indras before him and there would be many after him. Right at that very moment, in fact, there existed as many Indras in different realms as there were grains of sand on a beach. Each was trying to build a palace worthy of his glory but none was succeeding. Indras came and went with the seasons; and in the universe, which is a canvas of infinity, each Indra is eventually reduced to nothingness. Indra realized that in the denominator of infinity, which is the universe, he had no essential value.

The idea of 'value' (mulya), therefore, bothered the sages of India known as rishis. They kept asking what value meant if nothing matters when placed against the canvas of infinity. They observed nature carefully and passed on their learning through the Vedas and Puranas.

They observed that the elements fire, water and wind do not consume anything, for they 'value' nothing. Plants on the other hand value the elements, as they consume them in order to survive. Plants seek sunlight, they need air, they need water, they need the earth to survive and seek out valuable nutrients.

Thus, value is created when the consumer gives value to the commodity they consume. Plants give value to the elements by consuming them, animals give value to plants by consuming them, animals give value to other animals by consuming them. Food, the act of bhog or eating, creates value.

Humans consume everything: they consume plants, animals, minerals. We find value in everything and by consuming them we give value to nature around us and transform it into various commodities. The question, then, is what gives value to humans. Who consumes humans, who eats humans?

Now humans have found a very innovative way of creating value without being consumed physically, unlike plants and animals. We create value through the goods and services we exchange in the marketplace. This bestows value on us as providers. That is the unique capability of the human being.

Unlike animals whose bodies are consumed by their predators, humans create value that can be consumed by other human beings in the marketplace. Not only can we create value and exchange value, but we can also collect value. We can gather property. By gathering things, we give ourselves value.

In most societies, one is valued for the value one gathers, in terms of material prosperity. I am what I gather; I am what I have. Therefore, like Indra, we keep building and collecting more and more, becoming valued members in society who possess a lot of things.

The Vedas say that Artha is about generating food, by creating goods and services, while Kama is about satisfying this hunger. In Dharma, we consider the hunger of others and in Moksha, we outgrow our hunger. Only when we outgrow hunger can we be generous and charitable and let things go. Thus, rise the four pillars:

- Dharma (where we give value for others to consume)
- Artha (where we generate value)
- Kama (when we enjoy value)
- Moksha (when we outgrow the need to consume value)

Indra has not outgrown his hunger for things and therefore he is seeking value for himself by collecting things. Therefore, he is unable to be generous. He seeks value from the things he possesses. But in the Indian scheme of things, ultimately all things must be consumed.

Possessions do not give us value; wisdom gives us value. The realization that nothing lasts forever must help us in outgrowing our hunger. Only by satisfying other people's hunger do we truly bring value to society. Only when we outgrow our hunger can we be truly generous.

Neuroscientists are now observing that various hormones released in our body play a key role in our happiness, and these hormones are linked to the four Hindu pillars of meaning. For example, there is serotonin that is associated with happiness, and, in its absence, there is depression. There is dopamine that gives us a sense of exhilaration or achievement, and in its absence, there is a sense of worthlessness. There is oxytocin that is released during intimacy. There are various endorphins that are released during workouts, or when we are stressed, or when we laugh, that create a pleasurable feeling, comforting us.

Happiness is now seen as having many components: satisfaction, achievement, intimacy, comfort. It is being distinguished from pleasure. Pleasure is short-term. Happiness is long-term. Pleasure is individualistic. Happiness is social. Pleasure is seen as visceral, while happiness is seen as ethereal. One can get addicted to pleasure, but one cannot get addicted to happiness.

Pleasure is related with a release of dopamine and comes when there is sense of achievement. The more dopamine is released, the more we get addicted to it. We want more and more of it. This is what happens with drugs, like cocaine, that create an artificial sense of achievement, after which any other achievement falls short. Our craving for dopamine causes a situation where the brain fails to produce enough serotonin, as a result of which yearning for pleasure causes a decrease in general happiness. Hence, this results in depression.

This modern architecture of happiness mirrors the four-fold path of happiness prescribed in ancient Hindu scriptures. Dharma contributes to satisfaction; Artha to achievement, to exhilaration of success; Kama to pleasure and intimacy; Moksha to relief, resulting from letting go. We need a mixture of the four to be happy. And we realize that each of these four pillars of human meaning or purusha-arthas can be mapped to the happiness hormones identified by neuroscientists.

Dharma is about the other: giving back to society, feeding others, and taking care of those who need help, being responsible, being concerned about others, being a parent to the world at large. This is related to serotonin that can be called the dharma hormone.

Artha is about winning, about breaking boundaries, about reaching the goal, about surpassing the target. This makes dopamine the artha hormone. It is released when we go to the gym, when we do what our bosses expect us to do, when we meet a target, get work done on time, against all odds. It is the hormone of sport stars.

Kama is about intimacy, about desiring and being desired. It is linked to cozying up with family and friends, with children, with feeling safe. One can say that oxytocin is the kama hormone.

And how does one get rid of pain and suffering? The hormones which take away pain are endorphins, the moksha hormones, released when the body is stressed.

It is interesting that hormones related to pleasure, happiness, intimacy and comfort as per science can be easily mapped to the four goals of Hindu existence.

- Dharma releases serotonin
- Artha releases dopamine
- Kama releases oxytocin
- Moksha releases endorphin

One wonders whether the rishis were aware of these hormones intuitively or whether they were attentive enough to appreciate the architecture of happiness—that to live a balanced, fulfilled life, one needs good harmony between taking care of others, achieving material success, finding pleasure of intimacy and, finally, the ability to liberate oneself from worldly suffering.

Of course, not everyone will agree with this connection of neuroscience to the four Hindu pillars of happiness and not everyone will agree that the four Hindu pillars actually contribute to happiness, but that is okay...for

Within infinite myths lies an eternal truth
Who sees it all?
Varuna has but a thousand eyes
Indra, a hundred
You and I, only two.

Devdutt Pattanaik

DHARMA ARTHA KAMA MOKSHA

Dharma
Vedic Governance

The Aryans may have come to India through what is now Kazakhstan, with their proto-Sanskrit and horse-drawn chariots around 1500 BCE, but 'dharma' remains a very Indian word, in both pronunciation and meaning. The sound 'dh-' is unique to South Asia, which is why most people in the West, even in Iran (who are of Aryan descent), cannot pronounce 'dharma' the same way. And the meaning is based on Vedic metaphysics that locates humanity (purusha) in complementary tension with nature (prakriti), an indigenous idea.

But what does dharma mean? Scholars typically use adjectives like 'complex', 'obscure', 'subtle' and 'contextual' in order to define the word that suits their political leanings and social agenda. That's just lazy, if not manipulative.

The biggest problem emerges because English books typically

translate dharma as 'righteousness' or 'ethics and morality'. What is overlooked is that justice and ethics and morality come from cultural paradigms that are based on the idea of one life (Greco-Roman, Egyptian, Mesopotamian, Zoroastrian, Jewish, Christian, Islamic) whereas dharma presupposes REBIRTH!

When rebirth is your denominator, then karmic baggage comes into the present situation from the past, including past lives, and is carried forward to the future, and future lives. Failure to appreciate this fundamental Hindu paradigm of karma has resulted in a misunderstanding of dharma, and consequently Hinduism, by even the most well-meaning scholars.

The word 'dharma' first appears in the Rig Veda, but in a collection of a thousand hymns it occurs less than a hundred times, making it not a very key concept. It is related to 'foundation' and 'stability' and 'governance'. Even in the Upanishads, it is not a dominant theme.

The meaning is first explained rather clearly in Shatapatha Brahmana (800 BCE) which describes the absence of dharma as matsya nyaya, or fish law, the Hindu version of jungle law, where the mighty feed on the meek. This usually happens, we surmise from the verses, when there is lack of rain and scarcity, and most importantly, when there is no king (raja) to restrain anarchy (arajakta). This idea is further explained in the mythological story of Manu saving the small fish from the big fish and later the big fish saving Manu from the flood.

Dharma thus clearly indicates a situation where the mighty care for the meek. In a feudal system, it means the rich minority taking care of the poor majority. In a democracy it means the majority protecting the minority. This story of the fish being rescued resurfaces 1,200 years later in the Vishnu Purana (400 CE): the small fish becomes the first avatar of Vishnu, narratively conveying the idea of dharma.

The idea of dharma manifests in the Puranas too. In the Brahma Purana, we have the story of Brahma's sons, devas and asuras, who are constantly fighting. Swarga is the realm of devas, full of wealth and pleasure, ruled by Indra. But there is no peace, as it is constantly under siege by asuras, who live in Patala (under the ground), and are convinced they have been tricked out of their share of wealth. The battle of devas and asuras is unending. Indra is constantly replaced by more capable Indras, and asuras are constantly reborn with smarter boons that devas have to outsmart.

This is contrasted with Mount Kailash, the abode of Shiva, in the Shiva Purana, where there is always peace, as no one is hungry for anything: Shakti's tiger does not chase Shiva's bull who does not complain about the absence of grass on the icy mountain top. Kartikeya's peacock does not chase Shiva's snake which does not chase Ganesha's rat who does not eat Ganesha's sweets. So, while in Swarga, the hunger of devas is indulged and the hunger of asuras remains unsatisfied, in Kailash there is no hunger.

In Vaikuntha, the abode of Vishnu, in the Vishnu Purana, Vishnu is not hungry, but he seeks to satisfy the hunger of humanity by descending on earth in various forms (avatars) to teach humans dharma, first as a fish, and finally as an invader/revolutionary.

This brings us to the Ramayana, which is essentially a part of the Vishnu Purana, as it retells the story of Vishnu's avatar Ram, who lived in the Treta Yuga, so within the limits of time (kala). Here, we are told marriage is a way to establish dharma, and ensure the rights of husband and wife. But neither Surpanakha nor Ravana respect marriage laws and wish to satisfy their hunger (desire being a more refined word) at any cost. They think of themselves and not others. The royal siblings misuse their power to abuse the powerless exiled prince and his wife.

The Mahabharata, the other great epic, is also a part of the Vishnu Purana, as it retells the story of Vishnu's avatar Krishna, who lived in the Dvapara Yuga, also within the limits of time. Here, the complexity of the legal system is revealed. Who is the heir? Must the eldest be chosen over the youngest (Dhritarashtra over Pandu), the able-bodied over the disabled (Shantanu over Devapi), the bloodline (Kauravas) over the adopted (Pandavas)? It all comes down to: are the mighty (hundred brothers with eleven armies) willing to co-exist with the meek (five brothers with seven armies), or will they not share even 'a needlepoint of land'.

The idea that a king overturns matsya nyaya to establish dharma and prevent arajakta is found in the royal inscription that established the Pala kings of Bengal in 750 CE. Incidentally, Pala kings patronized Buddhism indicating that the concept of 'king overturning jungle law' is an Indian idea, not just a Hindu one.

The consistency in meaning from the Vedas through the

Puranas, from the epics to Buddhist lore, is remarkable.

Traditionally, in feudal societies, dharma is when the rich and powerful minority takes care of the poor and powerless majority. In a democracy, it is enacted when the numerically superior groups take care of minority groups.

However, today, in India, the majority Hindus are feeling threatened. Or their leaders are gaslighting them into victimhood. The minority has thus become the villain, whose demand for rights threatens the territories of the rich and the powerful. But are the majority actually rich and powerful? Or is that binary a convenient discourse?

In India, most people are poor and powerless. This vast majority of 'small fish' is being divided by the intellectual 'big fish' based on hereditary community privilege; and policies of positive discrimination are being unleashed in order to create a fair and just world. Unfortunately, the outcome reveals, the big fish are still eating the small fish, not just in India, but around the world, as we rely too much on policies rather than psychology.

Ancient Hindu sages knew that the human mind can bypass the noblest of rules. And so, the focus was less on policy (vidhi-anushthan) and more on the mind (mana). Dharma is not upholding the rules or breaking the rules—it is about genuinely caring for the meek and the weak. But that is sadly not something economists can measure. It remains what the Vedic rishis would call beyond attribute (nirguna), hence divine.

2

Artha
Yagna of Business

Business is a yagna, the ancient fire ritual described in Vedic scriptures. Into the flames, the yajaman makes offerings, exclaiming, 'Svaha!'—this of me I offer—hoping that the devata or deity he has invoked, satisfied with his offerings, emerges from the flames and says, 'Tathastu!'—as you wish.

Who is the yajaman? It is the shareholder who invests his resources and expects dividends in return; the employee who invests skills and expects a salary in return; the customer who invests a share of his wallet and expects products, services or ideas in return. Every exchange is a yagna. Anyone who initiates the exchange is the yajaman; anyone who closes the exchange is the devata. Svaha is the investment; tathastu is the return on investment. He who gives first then receives is the yajaman; he who receives first and then gives is the devata. In an ideal yagna, both yajaman and devata should be happy.

Management science restricts its gaze to svaha and tathastu: what is given and what is taken. These can be measured, hence managed. Everything begins with the outcome in sight, the desired tathastu; the svaha is designed accordingly. Great attention is paid to the offering, to the gestures, to the exclamations. No attention is paid to the yajaman or the devata. Their beliefs, feelings and fears cannot be measured, or managed, hence do not matter. Their presence is critical, but their personalities have no impact on the outcome. Both are relevant but replaceable. The yagna exists, independent of the gaze of the yajaman and devata.

In a traditional yagna, however, what matters most is the bhaav of the yajaman, the emotional intent underlying the ritual. This depends on how the yajaman sees the devata, which in turn depends on how he sees himself. The quality of the yagna depends on the gaze of the yajaman; this is shaped by the yajaman's beliefs, how he sees the world and himself. Should he be replaced by someone else, the belief will be different, the gaze will be different, hence the bhaav will be different. This will surely impact the outcome. The yagna thus has no independent existence outside the yajaman's subjective truth.

At a fast-food joint, management science prevails. Sadhana stands at the counter and speaks with a smile, in broken English, even when the customer does not understand English. Sadhana knows that the customer can speak Marathi, which she is fluent in, but she will continue to speak in English. She is following a process designed to create a particular customer experience. Every consumer is treated to the same consumer experience. Every employee is bound by the same rules. Individual prejudices and preferences are not allowed. Surely that is fair in the interests of standardization? But is she happy? Why does she feel dehumanized? Like she does not matter. Like only her obedience matters, not her intelligence. Yet she cannot complain because she is very well compensated. Why does she feel like a domesticated animal, not a fulfilled human? This is no yagna. She is neither yajaman, nor a devata. She is the karya-karta, who does what the karta tells her to do. This is not the Indian way. This is modern management, based on efficiency and effectiveness at the cost of humanity.

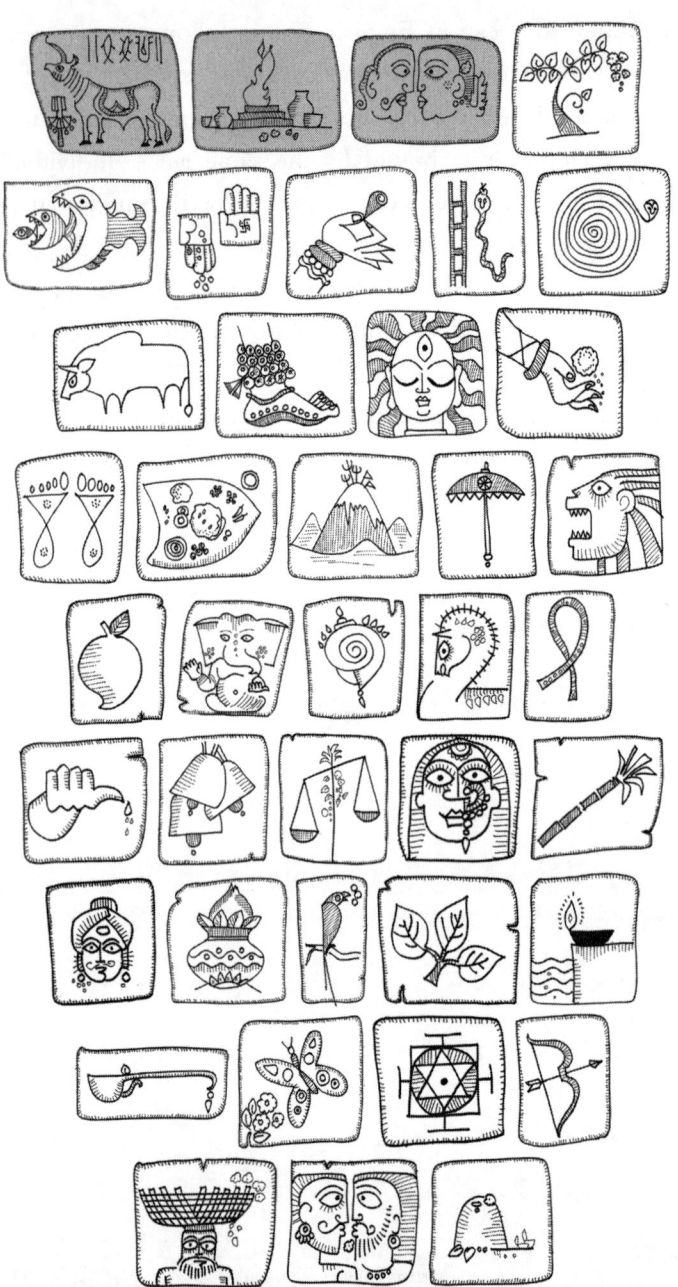

3

Kama
India's Erotic Tradition

About 1,500 years ago, a book called the *Kamasutra* came into being. The author, Vatsyayana, clarified that his knowledge was not original, that he had relied on many sources and authors to put it together. The original book is thought to have come from Shiva, as he explained the art of pleasure to his beloved, Shakti. It was brought from the realm of the gods to the realm of humans. Many authors then wrote about it and commented on it, and Vatsyayana finally prepared a compilation.

When you read the *Kamasutra*, you realize that it is not a guidebook on sex but a manual on how to live a pleasurable life. In fact, only 20 per cent of the *Kamasutra* deals with sexual activity. Most of the chapters are devoted to the philosophy and theory of love and desire. The book has around 1,200 verses. There are general chapters on how value is placed on three shastras of life, and not four. It speaks about Dharma Shastra, which relates to responsibility; Artha Shastra, which is about material success; and Kama Shastra, the pursuit of pleasure. It does not cover Moksha Shastra or spiritual freedom.

The *Kamasutra* tells us how a refined man should live and engage with friends, how his house should be designed so it can give him pleasure, and how he needs the help of allies to find lovers. Ten chapters of the book focus on the act of love, on erotica itself—the stimulation of desire, different kinds of embraces, caressing, kissing, biting, scratching, various copulatory positions, slapping, moaning, the behaviour of women and oral sex. It talks about foreplay and post-coital enjoyment.

Some sections even describe how to find a spouse and make her comfortable on the wedding night, something which most Indian men seem to have forgotten about. The book discusses the relationship between multiple wives of a man and his equation with each of them. It also talks about extramarital affairs and how to deal with them in a non-moralistic way; it even contains references to go-betweens and secret passages through which men can meet their lovers, who were wives of other men.

There are chapters on courtesans. Unlike extramarital affairs, visits to courtesans by married men were not frowned upon. Courtesans got to meet different types of men and in exchange, they provided sexual and sensual company. Some chapters describe magical rituals to enhance or replenish the sexual virility of men. The *Kamasutra* is an exciting text of its time, covering the subject of sex in a practical manner. There is no condemnation of sex with courtesans and partners of other men, or polygamy. We see a very different world in the book than the one we live in, where sex itself has come to be seen as a shameful act and where women have to submit to men. This is reflected, for instance, in many modern movie songs that glamorize men who behave like predators.

In the fifteenth century, when Lodhi kings ruled Delhi, a sex manual called the *Ananga Ranga* was written. Its purpose was very different: it taught men how to satisfy their wives, so the latter remained faithful in the marriage. The story goes that a naked woman once walked into the king's court and asked if there was any courtier who could satisfy her sexually. Koka Shastri was the man who succeeded in the endeavour. The king was pleased and asked Koka Shastri to draft a manual on ways to fulfil women's physical needs.

In the *Ananga Ranga*, men and women—their bodies, sexual organs and temperaments—are classified differently. Various frameworks have been provided to match the right kind of man with the right kind of woman. Different ways through which men and women can pleasure each other are also listed. Interestingly, the *Ananga Ranga*, like the *Kamasutra*, contains information about alchemical aphrodisiacs for increased virility, and it also describes how astrology can play a role in lovemaking and in igniting love and passion.

These are the erotic traditions of India that no modern

government will include in school or college curriculums. We are made to feel ashamed for having sexual desires in a world which is increasingly being dominated by celibate men who claim to be holy.

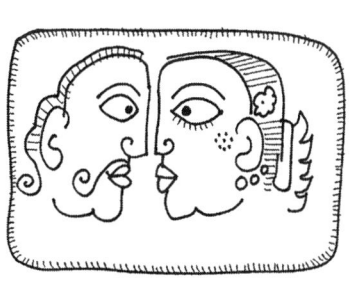

4

Moksha
Karma Is Not
'As You Sow, So Shall You Reap'

Say the word 'swastika' in a global workplace, and you are likely to be branded a Nazi. Few, if any, will equate it to 'su-asti'—let good things happen—a very common Sanskrit phrase used in Hindu rituals. In fact, in Bali, Indonesia, the standard greeting of local Hindus is 'Om Suwasti-astu'. The West always decides what words should mean what in the global arena. So, swastika is what Hitler decided it was. 'Avatar' is what James Cameron decided it was. And 'karma' is what Western journalists decided it should be.

Words like karma discomfort the West. It equates karma with destiny and accuses Indians of being fatalistic and complacent because of their faith in karma. Such views are based not on a wrong understanding but an incomplete understanding of karma. It is more based on the biblical phrase 'as you sow, so shall you reap' and less on the Gita phrase, 'focus on action, not results'. A deeper understanding of karma will reveal it is also the force that makes us extremely proactive and responsible BEFORE the result, and fatalistic AFTER the result.

The word karma first occurs in the Rig Samhita, the earliest collection of Vedic verses. But there it means activity, specifically ritual activity. It is not related to consequence of action. In other words, it means action, but not reaction. In the Vedas, karma means sowing the seed.

In the later texts, the Upanishads, it also means the production of the subsequent fruit. This latter meaning is perhaps embedded in the early use of the word too, because the early use of the word karma occurs in the context of yagna and yagna is performed to seek a 'reaction from the devas'. Yagna involves svaha (input) of humans that results in tathastu (output) from the gods.

This shift of meaning in karma, from mere action to action that causes reaction, is attributed to shramanas (thinkers) who refused to be mere brahmanas (ritual doers). They lived around 500 BCE, known as the Axis Age, the age that also saw the rise of Socratic thought in Greece, Confucian thought in China and Zoroastrian thought in Persia.

The thinkers of India included men like Yagnavalkya who was married to two women, and Sakyamuni Buddha and Vardhamana Mahavira, both of whom gave up marriage and family to become monks. Yagnavalkya, despite his radical thoughts, did not break free from the Brahmanical ritual fold of household, and was hence deemed an astika, one who believes in the value of the yagna and the household. Buddha started the Buddhist monastic order while Mahavira was seen as a leader of the much older, austere Jain order. Both of them were called nastikas, those who do not value the Vedic practice of maintaining the sacred household fires for humans, gods and ancestors.

Brahmans preferred to see Kshatriyas (kings, landowners) as their primary patrons. So the Vaishyas (mercantile community) gave patronage to the shramanas. These merchants perhaps contributed to the understanding of karma, for much of karma theory resonates in trading practices, such as balance sheet, debt and return on investment. Every action came to be seen eventually as an input, for which an output was demanded. Good investments meant good returns; bad investments meant bad returns.

But who knows what action is good and what action is bad? Yes, karma may be about reaping the fruit of the seed we sow, but you may think you are sowing the seed of a sweet mango when it is quite possible that the fruit will turn out to be a sour tamarind or a fiery chilly.

A king was once given a fruit that if consumed by his wife would enable her to bear him a child. The king had two wives, so he gave each one half of the fruit. As a result, both queens gave birth to half a child. Thus, the action (dividing the fruit to be fair to both wives) was good but the reaction (half a child from each wife) was bad.

Likewise, a thief who climbed the high branches of a tree to escape the police was blessed by a deity, because flowers from the tree accidentally fell on an image of the deity that was right under the tree. This makes karma unpredictable, much like market investments.

People have long tried to classify actions as good karma and bad karma, but the fact is that paap (bad actions) are usually called so in hindsight, when the outcome is negative. Likewise, punya (good actions) become so in hindsight, when the outcome is positive. At the time of action, we do not know whether the results will favour us or not. We thus only have control on our actions, not on the reactions, or how the future will judge our actions. This point is amplified by Krishna in the Bhagavad Gita in response to Arjuna's query about karma.

Karma presupposes rebirth. Our current situation in life is a reaction to actions in the past life. That is why some people are born poor, ugly or to horrible parents. The West often points to this belief as the cause of India's complacency, that by attributing current circumstances to fate, rather than to social injustice, there is no motivation to strive or fight. What is overlooked is that the word 'fate' comes from the Fates, three Greek goddesses who spun the yarn of mortal life and who, on the advice of Zeus, king of all Olympian gods, determined how long the thread should be, and when it should be cut.

Those who genuinely believe in karma know that just as the past determines the present, the present determines the future. Thus, to secure the future, one must work really hard in the present. In other words, genuine belief in karma should make a person more proactive and responsible. If a person chooses to be lazy instead, it has nothing to do with karmic philosophy and everything to do with laziness.

In fact, the idea of karma yoga originated to counter monastic practices that were seen as promoting inaction (renunciation). Philosophies were elaborated to cope with the fear of karmic consequence and enable man to perform his duties as a householder. These philosophies declared that inaction was also an action, that an act of omission had its own consequences. He who fought could kill the killer. He who did not fight enabled the killer to strike another victim. Thus, no monk could escape from karma. To liberate oneself from the web of karma, one had to develop the mental equilibrium to exist in worldly circumstances, aware but unperturbed by good or bad circumstances and outcomes.

The West rejects the idea of rebirth. Both the religious and rational West believes that a child is born with a clean karmic balance sheet. That when a person dies the balance sheet ceases to exist. There is absolutely no other life where this is carried forward.

Not so in Hinduism, Buddhism and Jainism, where there is an outstanding balance at the time of birth and an outstanding balance at the time of death. The former comes from the previous life and the latter leads to the next life. Thus, karma determines the current circumstances of our life.

How we choose to react to past karma is our choice. We may choose to accept it or change it. Our choices may be deemed good by some and bad by others, right by some, wrong by others, but these ethical and moral qualifications have no impact on the consequences of our actions, and the impact on our future circumstances. Whatever has to happen, will happen, our desires notwithstanding.

The West—with its obsession with empiricism, certainty and predictability—finds such Indian explanations of karma exasperating. Thus, it rejects all Indian definitions, and prefers simplistic Western ones. We have to learn to distinguish the two.

5

Dharma
Law of the Fish

The Vishnu Purana begins with the story of the Matsya Avatar, the fish incarnation of Vishnu. A tiny fish approaches Manu, the first leader of mankind, on the riverbank and begs him to save it from the big fish. Manu, in his compassion, scoops the tiny fish out of the river in the palm of his hand and puts it in a pot. The tiny fish is immensely grateful. But the next day the tiny fish has grown in size and the pot is too small to accommodate it. Manu transfers the fish to a bigger pot. A day later, the fish has grown once again. Manu has to move it to a giant pitcher. A day later that too is not enough.

So, the fish is moved from the pitcher to a pond, from the pond to a lake, from the lake to a river and finally to the sea. Soon, even the sea is not expansive enough. Rains start to fall so that the ocean can expand to make room for the fish. As the ocean expands, the waters creep over the earth and Manu realizes that the whole world will soon be submerged by the rising waters. The rain continues to fall, the sea continues to rise, making more and more room for the fish.

Manu cries out in alarm and wonders what is happening. The fish smiles and transforms into Vishnu, and promises to save Manu from the flood. It asks Manu to take refuge in a boat, with enough room for himself, his family, various animals and plants and the seven wise sages in whose custody rests the wisdom of the world (the Hindu Noah's Ark, some may say). The giant fish then guides this boat through the rain and storm to the peak of Mount Meru, the only piece of land that survives the Great Flood.

Why does Vishnu take the form of a fish for his first interaction with mankind? To understand this, one must first understand the Sanskrit phrase 'matsya nyaya' or 'law of the fishes', whose loose equivalent in English, as I mentioned, is 'law of the jungle'. In the story, the tiny fish asks Manu to save him from the big fish. But in nature (the jungle), no one is going to come to the aid of the tiny fish because everyone is on their own and only the fit survive.

Manu, however, is human and not entirely part of nature. He has been given the faculty by which he can defy the law of the jungle. That is what makes man human. Manu acts, not from the need to survive, but out of compassion. The moment he scoops the fish out and saves it, civilization is born: a place where even the weakest can thrive. The laws instituted to make this happen are dharma, making matsya

Dharma Artha Kama Moksha

nyaya the very opposite—adharma.

A government is like Manu: trying to create (through its laws and regulations) a system where the weakest can thrive and the strong don't dominate the weak. They don't want large MNCs and business houses (the big fish) to establish a monopoly and seize control of the market. They want the smaller players to thrive too. Hence, they impose regulations and licenses and laws and do everything in their power to stamp out a market where anything goes.

Such actions by the government, destroying the 'free' market and stifling laissez-faire, have been repeatedly denounced. But they are necessary, since man, while capable of extreme generosity, is also capable of extreme greed. Government laws and regulations and licenses are needed to protect the interests of the weaker sections of society, to ensure a fair distribution of wealth.

The tiny fish, however, does not remain a tiny fish forever. It grows in size. Unable to provide for itself, totally dependent on Manu, it begs for more: a bigger pot, a bigger pond. And Manu, in his compassion, keeps giving and giving and giving, until finally even the sea is not big enough for the fish. Rains must come and the sea must expand so that the fish can be accommodated. In the process Manu's world is destroyed.

Thus, the story shows the price of foolhardy compassion. Neither Manu nor the fish are willing to face a truth—that the fish is no longer helpless. Manu, because he is afraid of being seen as less compassionate; the fish, because it is afraid of fending for itself.

This has happened in India where laws and regulations and licenses ended up stifling growth, and destroying the economy. The rules had to be changed. The markets had to open up to foreign investments. Manu had to let the fish help itself. But that has not been taken kindly. Everywhere we see protests, riots, marches against the opening up of the Indian economy. The fish is afraid and is lashing out at Manu, who perhaps never prepared the fish for this moment.

A leader is like Manu. While creating more markets, he has to consciously invest sometimes disproportionately higher amounts in smaller, developing markets over large, developed ones. In the absence of such concerted effort, the budget can be totally appropriated by the big sales team managing the developed markets with its grand promises, leaving the small sales team with little or no budget.

A good leader never asks the smaller markets for immediate returns. The bigger markets may cry foul and taunt the leader with proof that if more investments were made it could perhaps cough up a bigger return. But the leader's vision is long-term. The big market may not be big forever and the small market will eventually grow. For the moment, the tiny fish needs its pot and pond, and the big fish can manage in the sea.

But a shrewd leader must be wary of the plan becoming a habit. The developing market can choose to call itself a developing market forever. It is possible that nobody has noticed that it has become a developed market, that it does not need that extra care it was given initially, that it now has the power to play with the big boys. A wise leader should always keep an eye on the size of the fish and know when it is time to throw it back into the sea. Good leadership is about capacity building. A good leader is not someone who gives you the fish—he is one who teaches you how to fish. That is the first lesson of the Vishnu Purana.

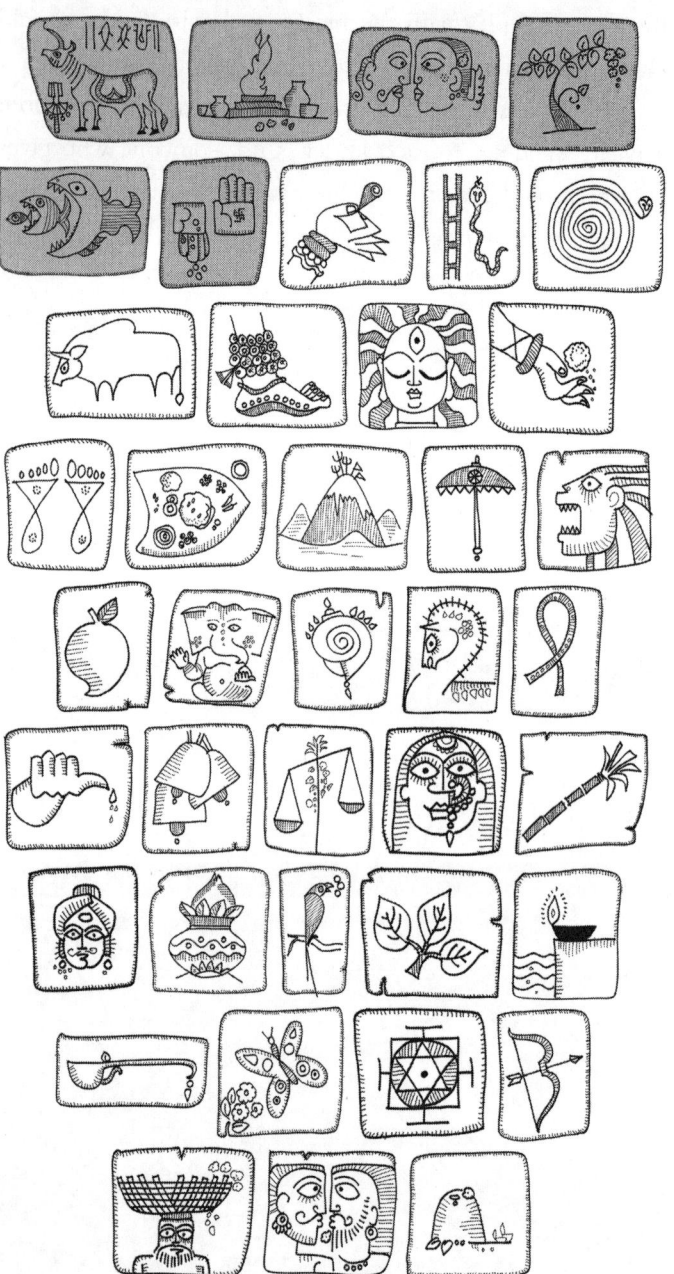

6

Artha
Architecture of Fear

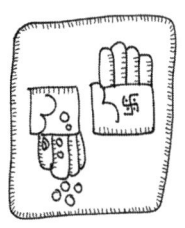

Why do we buy things we don't really need? Why do we seek control over things and people? Why do we seek predictability in business? Why do we love brands? If we wish to answer this 'why', we have to move into the realm of psychology and understand the origins of fear. A more acceptable term for fear in the corporate world is 'stress'. The word fear does not go well with the corporate image of a valorous, confident warrior, dressed in a smart black suit, tablet in hand.

Every Hindu god and goddess raises his or her palm in a gesture which means 'do not be afraid' (a-bhaya), indicating that the ancients knew the role of fear in day-to-day life. If there was no fear (bhaya), there would be no hunger or desire (bhook), hence no desire to consume (bhoga). Our desire to consume results in a heavy toll on resources (bali) for which we have to pay a price (karma).

Thus, fear is the seed of all the issues we face in the business world—from demand to supply, transparency and governance. It is fear that shapes our relationship with consumers, auditors, authorities, bosses, processes. Yet, this is not part of business school curriculums, perhaps because we are over-reliant on human reason and forget that humans are essentially not reasonable but rather insecure and frightened.

Stress or fear can be traced to the first life form (sajiva). Unlike inanimate objects (ajiva), it was determined to survive, fight for its life and avoid death by seeking nutrition from the earth around. As more life forms emerged, everyone competed for food. Mutation took place and diversity emerged to improve chances of survival. The greatest mutation was the split between life-forms that move (chara) and life-forms that do not move (achara), meaning animals and plants. A plant grows towards food, but it cannot run from predators that feed on it. An animal can both run towards food and away from predators.

In animals we see the fear inherent in the food chain: the fear in prey of being hunted and the fear in predators of starvation. The other fear that is superimposed is that of the pecking order: who will be alpha and hence get access to the most food and most mates. The one at the bottom of the pyramid is at a disadvantage, especially the male, who gets least food and probably no mate. Can this be the reason for the aggression seen in men?

Dharma Artha Kama Moksha

But humans are the most unique life-form. We have a mind that can imagine (manas) and so we imagine who we are and wonder if others imagine themselves the same way. This creates anxiety, the fear of invalidation. We seek status and justification and most importantly meaning (artha). We seek nourishment for our self-image and are constantly protecting this self-image from rivals and predators. This constitutes our architecture of fear.

It is significant that the word artha-shastra simultaneously means economics (do we generate and distribute enough wealth, income, revenue?), politics (do we get enough power to compete, catch prey, shun predators?), and philosophy (do we know who we really are, live meaningful lives?). This was a holistic approach to business and management, restricted not just to building efficient money-making businesses but locating business in society, and even the cosmos. One finds this critical understanding missing in students emerging from the best universities in the world. They are skilled warriors but clueless about what they are fighting for. And this cluelessness results in strange, even dangerous behaviour.

Let us take three examples of behaviour found in the corporate world to demonstrate the key role of the fear-seed in business activities:

- Consumers and vendors constantly seek deals and discounts. It makes them feel powerful. Shopping becomes retail therapy, a chance to feel significant in a world that does not care for you. Service-providers realize the value of making a customer feel valuable. Fear is intensified by creating hierarchies amongst customers: you are a level 1 customer, level 2 customer or level 3 customer. Depending on the hierarchy you get a different level of service. Your waiting time is less if you are more loyal and/or have more spending power.

- A senior manager finds himself being continuously judged. The auditors judge the processes he follows. The bosses judge his performance. He is constantly being told what he has not achieved and how he is not adequately aligned. He discovers his compensation is never good enough, always lesser than his rivals, and this poor compensation is always rationalized and justified during appraisal time. He is repeatedly told, in quarter after quarter, he has to be better, run faster. He has to stay the ever-hungry predator who is never allowed to rest and play, to satisfy the insatiable hunger of the anonymous institutional shareholder.

- A very successful investment banker wonders if people he meets know how smart he is. So, he buys the best car, the best house, throws the best parties, goes on the finest holidays, brags about how he works for only an hour a day, or maybe an hour a week, constantly highlights his brilliance, and even does charity, because he wants to succeed in the sphere of social responsibility too. Finally, he starts seeing value in possessing a bathtub made of gold. Or gets a kick in getting freebies like celebrities.

An understanding of fear is critical in management if one accepts that humans are animals with imagination, who cannot be domesticated using reason. Desire, greed, ambition, control, success, compliance—all these factors impact a person's architecture of fear. We look at institutions to raise their palm and display the symbol of a-bhaya. Instead, their massive size, steel-and-glass coldness, impersonal business processes, card-swipe machines and closed-circuit TVs only amplify the bhaya.

7

Kama
Contribution of the Courtesans

In ancient Tamil epics such as the *Silappadikaram* and *Manimeghalai*, we find a description of three kinds of women.

Women such as Kannagi, who were chaste and devoted to a single man (even if the man had many wives); women such as Manimeghalai, who kept away from men and lived as nuns; and the third kind, such as Madhavi, women who had multiple lovers and were attached to no single man. In later times, such women were considered the wives of a temple deity or devadasis, who saw their god in all their lovers. This last category of women has often been described in modern literature as ancient sex workers or prostitutes or sacred concubines.

We refuse to see them as single women who indulged in the profession of entertainment, by being singers and dancers.

They were known as 'nats' and 'natis', or entertainers, who chose not to be bound to a single man and had multiple lovers. They were part of matrilineal clans, where the property and inheritance passed on from mother to daughter.

Instead of accepting their lifestyle as different, society has condemned them. Their lifestyle has been reduced to the term prostitution and therefore we refuse to see this as one of the many types of diverse community structures which thrived, and was given due importance, in ancient India.

The idea of beautiful women who are well versed in the arts and bound to no single man emerges in mythology in the references to apsaras. In the Rig Samhita, the apsaras reside in the paradise known as Swarga, which human males crave and pine for. But these apsaras are known to be capricious and lose interest after some time and detach themselves from human beings. They are uninterested in the concept of fidelity. Even when they bear offspring, they are not attached to the children and leave them behind, at times even on the forest floor. In other words, these are free women. The Puranas state that when devas and asuras churned the ocean of milk, Lakshmi, the goddess of fortune, emerged and, with her arose the apsaras who made the heavens their abode and entertained the gods.

In later Nath traditions, these free women were considered to be yoginis and dakinis who lived in plantain forests: a plantain being a metaphor for women. It is said that the plantain grove was the realm of witches who stripped men of their masculinity and trapped them in the world of mortality. It was a world dreaded by the monastic order. The monks feared them as creatures who stripped men of wealth and power and captured these for themselves.

In early Buddhist literature, too, courtesans such as Amrapali and Vasavadatta played a very important role. We are told that many of them were so rich that they gifted groves, houses, food and wealth to many Buddhist monks and even to the Buddha. But in later literature, such as Vinaya Pitaka and the Puranas, we find a discomfort with these women; they are considered temptations, destroying concentration and waylaying the ascetic. While in Hindu literature Indra sends apsaras such as Menaka from paradise to distract rishis like Vishwamitra from gaining spiritual power, their images are carved into temple walls.

All this reveals a social tension between the ascetic and artistic traditions, the hermit and the entertainer, the former being more masculine and the latter more feminine.

When Islam came to India, courtesans continued to thrive in the form of the tawaifs. They played a very important role in the rise of classical Indian music and dance. In temples across India, there were vast communities of women associated with music, dance and the arts. These women were considered to be exponents of the sixty-four different kinds of arts, which meant many of them were literate, well-versed in poetry and prose. We know of famous courtesans who wrote poetry, and still others who found renown as exponents of various musical forms.

The arrival of the British changed all that. Along with the British, especially in Victorian times, came a colonial morality and an idea of virtue. Anything associated with sex and sexuality was condemned as being evil and wrong. Unsurprisingly, the ones to suffer the most was this community of independent women artists.

Incredibly, modern Hindu puritans mimicked Victorian Puritanism and saw puritanical fanaticism as 'tradition'. Hindu reformists from the Arya Samaj to the Brahmo Samaj tried to change Hinduism and align it with Christianity. Temple worship was frowned upon as it was seen as idolatry. Krishna worship overlooked or rationalized the erotic nature of songs in the *Gita-Govinda*. Subsequently, with Christian puritanical doctrine, these women were perceived to be stains on Hindu culture. Thus began the Anti-Nautch movement of the nineteenth century, a systematic movement to destroy these independent women by reducing their role in society to prostitution and, consequently, condemning and shunning them.

The idea of the independent woman as someone to be feared continues to this date. We can see clearly, on the internet, how single women are targeted by trolls. These trolls typically use sexual metaphors and see freethinking women as loose, rather than as autonomous beings in control of their own bodies. In doing so, we have denied the grand contribution of women artists and entrepreneurs to Indian culture—and that is unfortunate.

8

Moksha
Karmic Balance

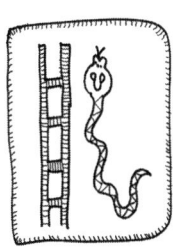

Most of us have played the board game snakes and ladders. The throw of dice forces you to move a number of steps forward. The point you reach on the board could have a picture of a snake or a ladder, or it could be empty. If it is the mouth of the snake, then you tumble down. If it is the base of a ladder, you are catapulted several steps ahead. If it is neither, then you wait for the next throw of dice to move forward (or backward). The only thing that is in our hand is the throw of the dice. Everything else is luck, determined by the presence or absence of a snake or ladder.

Fortune and misfortune are thus not in our hands but determined by forces we have no control over. And we really cannot manipulate the throw of the dice. So effectively, nothing in the game is in our control. Known as gyan-chauper or moksha-patam, this game was created hundreds of years ago by either Jain monks or Hindu sages to explain the concept of karma.

Of course, it can be very depressing to know that our action (throwing of the dice) is a gamble and the outcome of snakes and ladders is also a gamble. Everything is a gamble. It makes us feel helpless, like riding in a car with no gears or brakes. Could that be life?

Naturally, one does not want to play such a game. But that is inaction. No participation, no engagement, no fun, no connection with the other players of the game. That is the hermit's choice: to watch others play the game, mock their excitement and frustration at the outcome. But the wise householder, who has the wisdom of the hermit, participates in the game without getting attached to the results. He enjoys the game for itself, knowing that victory and defeat are determined by factors that are not in his control. It is all a game of probability.

The snake of misfortune that pushes us back is opposed by the ladder of fortune that pushes us ahead. Sometimes, the tail of the snake lands us just a step away from a ladder. Thus, fortune lurks in the corner of misfortune and vice versa. We never know what will come our way. Life is full of surprises, an adventure for all.

Where did the snakes and ladders come from? We are told it is karma, the process of nature, created by a whole set of actions and reactions. An accumulation of good deeds results in a ladder and an accumulation of bad deeds creates the snake. How can we do more good deeds and fewer bad deeds? No one knows. All we have in our hands is the dice, the throwing of which remains the same, whether it lands in the snake's mouth or at the base of a ladder. There is no way to determine if an action is good or bad or if its reaction will be good or bad.

In the game of snakes and ladders, we can ride a wave and the wave can take us up or down. It is created by a host of natural forces. We merely ride it. We delude ourselves that we have created the wave. As Krishna reminds us in the Bhagavad Gita, 'You are not the doer. Nature is the doer. You are just the observer.'

We can say that our life is a karmic balance sheet, a set of fortunes and misfortunes, determined by past and present actions. But the sages keep mum on that. For no one really knows how our life is shaped. Some believe we create our fortune through action. Some believe our fortune is created by our past deeds. Or maybe, no one really plans or controls this roller-coaster game of snakes and ladders. All we have control over is how we perceive the experience. Are we excited by fortune and disappointed by misfortune? Do we think we created the fortune or misfortune? Do we feel the world, God, nature or the game, owes us this fortune or misfortune?

Moksha is realizing that the world may essentially be beyond human control, but not our emotions. We can try and control the game, manipulate our moves and our victories, and rationalize the events of the world. We can grant ourselves value as victims who have been tortured by the game or heroes who have conquered the game.

Or we can just accept that it is a game that everyone plays. Sometimes we are in, sometimes we are out. Sometimes we slip down and sometimes we rise up. The fun part is observing our emotions and those of the other players. And making friends across the board game we call life.

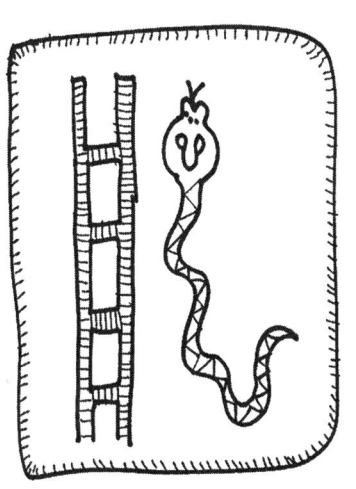

9

Dharma
Finite to Infinite

The concept of 'values' is an integral part of the corporate world. And every corporation, even the most corrupt, has 'values' printed on its annual general report. This can be traced to the notion of 'commandments' which comes from Abrahamic mythology, wherein the God of Abraham put down a set of rules (and values, when there are no rules) of how humans are supposed to live their lives. This set of rules is transmitted by messengers known as prophets.

Sadly, no one is sure what the correct rules and values are which is why Jewish people fight with Muslims and Muslims fight with Christians. And there are fights between various Jewish, Islamic and Christian subgroups. The 'secular' nation state simply replaces God with 'We, the People' or the 'State' and uses the same model of governance based on rules/

values that everyone is supposed to follow.

The Vedas look at the world differently. As we study the transformation of Hinduism from Vedic to Puranic times, we notice an obsession with concepts such as infinity (ananta), diversity (aneka) and impermanence (anitya). This is the very opposite of Abrahamic or Semitic thought which seeks to 'fix' the world by a set of fixed 'rules/values'.

For the Vedas, nature came first, before culture, before humans even. And nature, as we have seen, functions as per the 'law of jungle', where might is right, only the fittest survive, and driven by their hunger and fear animals establish food chains, pecking orders and territories.

Humans don't have to subscribe to this jungle way, thanks to our ability to imagine. We can help the helpless. We can provide resources to help the unfit survive. We don't have to form packs or herds. We don't have to dominate or be territorial.

We can use our imagination to outgrow our hunger and fear, and help others cope with their hunger and fear as well. Humans have the ability to think of others (para-atma) and so can reach the infinite divine (param-atma) beyond the self (jiva-atma). When we do that, we are in line with our potential. This is dharma. When we don't do that, when we are not in line with our potential, we are following adharma.

In the Vedic worldview, the focus is not on rules/values and obedience and punishment. The focus is on engaging with others with awareness and working towards reducing our hunger and fear. High hunger and fear nourish ego or aham, and take us away from divinity or atma. When humans seek to dominate and control other people for self-aggrandizement, it is aham at work. When we enable people to empathize with each other, and seek to make them happy, rather than defeat and control others, then atma is at work. Rules/values are just hygiene.

And so, in the Ramayana, we have the rule-abiding hero (Ram) and a rule-breaking villain (Ravana), and in the Mahabharata we have a rule-breaking hero (Krishna) and a rule-abiding villain (Duryodhana). The problem is not the rules/values. The problem is not obedience or disobedience. The problem is 'where are you coming from', 'what is your intent'. Are you working only for self (jiva-atma) or are you concerned about the other (para-atma)? Ram and Krishna work for others, Ravana and Duryodhana work for the self. We are all in between, hopefully moving towards dharma and atma (Ram/Krishna).

10

Artha
Violence of Enterprise

M any people are of the opinion that eating vegetarian food is indicative of kindness and non-violence. That is not so. Ask the bull, or rather the bullock.

A bullock is a castrated bull: a bull whose testicles have been cut so as to deprive him of male hormones that make him untamable and violent. In other words, a bullock is to a bull is what a eunuch is to a man. 'Gelding', 'neutering' and 'banding' are nicer words used instead of castration. It's a brutal procedure carried out all over the world, turning the virile bull into a eunuch-bull so that it can serve as a beast of burden. Since buffalo males cannot serve as beasts of burden, as bulls do, they were just sacrificed in ritual ceremonies and offered to Durga and Kali. Hence the concept of 'buffalo-demon' and not 'bull-demon' as the castrated bull had the economic benefit of pulling carts and ploughs.

Indian civilization owes a lot to the bullock. For 5,000 years, maybe more, bullocks have been used in the Indian subcontinent to plough fields and pull carts, enabling the production and transport of grains, pulses, fruits and vegetables. Bulls were known and venerated in the Harappan civilization. Their image has been found on clay seals. Clay carts found in the archaeological sites indicate that they knew how to castrate aggressive bulls and turn them into docile bullocks.

In Vedic times, men displayed their strength and agility by fighting or dancing with or leaping over aggressive, snorting bulls. In the Bhagavata Purana, there is a reference to Krishna, the divine cowherd, overpowering seven wild bulls to win the hand of the princess Satya in marriage. Such practices are still popular in many agricultural communities though animal rights activists have sought to ban them.

Unless castrated, a bull cannot be used as a beast of burden. Castration has very much been in the news lately. Some judges in India believe that the threat of castration is enough to protect children and women from sexual abuse: so deep is the fear of castration in the male psyche. Most men consider it a fate worse than death.

Once castrated, a bull cannot be used for mating and if there is no mating then a cow cannot get pregnant, hence cannot give birth to more calves, and so cannot give milk. So for the sake of milk, at least some bulls are not castrated. They are allowed to roam free in the village streets and farms. These untamed masculine creatures are even worshipped as Shiva's bull, Nandi, whose proud genitals are on display in every Shiva temple, and which contain the seed that eventually leads to the production of milk. Nandi embodies Shiva's virility as well as his independent and untamable nature.

In modern sanitized temples, you will find images of Nandi without testicles on display as the practice embarrasses the modern urban devotee, who often does not know the difference between a bull, a bullock, and sometimes even a cow. This is why cow protection also means the protection of bulls and bullocks and barren cows. Gender nuance is completely lost. While protection of the milk-giving cow has a strong economic basis, the protection of bulls and bullocks and barren cows is purely political—a belligerent stand that is beyond reason and so best left alone, as angry bulls often are.

Every time people speak of how vegetarianism is linked to non-violence and kindness, I think of the millions of bulls who over India's history have been castrated to plough fields and pull carts. Is that cruelty or not? Is that violence or not? Who carries the karmic burden of the violence? The farmer or the consumer?

Civilization is built on violence. We can argue which form of violence is acceptable and which form of violence is valid. But humans can never ever escape violence. Violently, we destroy forests and change the course of rivers, and bore into mountains to create human settlements and farms. In the process, vast ecosystems are destroyed, killing millions of birds and beasts and fish and insects. Since we do not witness these killings, we assume they do not happen.

The act of eating is violent because embedded in cultivated food (not the wild foraged food of ascetics) is the killing and castration of some animal or the other. Jain sages realized this and introduced fasting as a technique to reduce the karmic burden. They insisted on eating only fruit that fell from trees naturally, not fruit that was plucked. Even this, they realized, meant depriving some other animal of food. Only one who could truly give up hunger could overcome the violence associated with the consumption of food. Such an evolved being was 'bhagavat', worthy of worship. Every other form of fasting is to remind us how difficult it is to escape the karmic burden of samsara or civilization.

Our understanding of violence today is very poor. We actually believe that we can have a culture without it. This poor understanding of human culture is the result of increasingly outsourcing violence to farmers and soldiers and butchers, and to machines and robots, and to terrorists and goons.

Without violence, farms cannot be established. Without violence, produce cannot be protected from pests. From violence comes food on our table. If you seek food, if you seek to feed others, you are involved in some form of violence. This violence is very visible in the consumption of non-vegetarian food. The violence is invisible, and outsourced, if you are consuming vegetarian food. Since everyone consumes vegetables and grains and cereals and pulses, everyone is responsible for creating a demand that involves farmers chopping the testicles of baby male calves. We can argue endlessly how much violence is acceptable. That is like arguing how much wealth is acceptable, where the rich will never agree with the poor. We can also argue that castration of a bull is not actually violence, or at least better than death. I wonder how many bullocks would agree to that.

11

Kama
Audience Is Customer

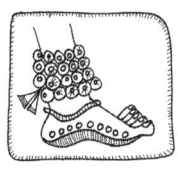 I have noticed that in a Western classical music or dance performance, the presence or absence of quality in the audience makes no difference to the quality of the performance. It is 'one way'. But in an Indian classical music or dance performance, the artiste blooms as the audience responds to their performance. The artiste churns rasa (aesthetic juice) in the senses and the hearts of the audience through the performance. She offers bhoga (food) to satisfy their craving. Their attention and adulation contributes to the quality of the performance. Finally, they 'burp' in satisfaction. Then they pay her with appreciation, adulation, praise and, of course, money. Thus, it is a two-way relationship.

A few months ago, I attended just such a fabulous Marathi show that spoke about a little-known yet widely prevalent subculture of traditional singers and dancers in Maharashtra who perform only at private gatherings. It gave me a glimpse into the dancing halls and the world of dancing girls, popularly known as 'nautch girls', before they were termed dirty, condemned by British colonizers and many puritan Hindus in the nineteenth and twentieth centuries. It was in these private performing spaces that the arts continued to flourish in India: here, song and dance were cultivated way before the modern classifications of folk, popular and classical.

This was the world of the 'nat', the performer, a special kind: not one who was attached to a temple, nor one who sought audiences like a travelling bard or an itinerant performer, but one who got audiences to seek him/her out. During the performance, the performer said, 'But we don't have audiences. We have customers!' And with that one sentence, I realized she was revealing one of the deepest secrets of Natya-Shastra, the Indian theory of performing arts, that makes Indian performance art rather unique. She revealed the two-way relationship between the performer and audience, which is not just sensory, emotional or intellectual, but also commercial.

The word 'customer' bothers us. When a dancing girl says 'customer', we automatically assume that she is a prostitute. An artiste can have an audience, not customers. An artiste strikes a commercial transaction with buyers, but somehow art is not seen as 'consumption' for a 'customer'. Art is made ethereal by differentiating 'commercial art' from 'pure art'. This is an outcome of Puritanism, a mixture of Victorian as well as Buddhist, Jain or Hindu monastic values, where money is seen as a bad, corrupting influence. Even worse is the idea that pleasure can be part of transactions.

Yet, pleasure is also a commodity that can be sold in the market. The performer exists to satisfy sensory, emotional, intellectual and even physical cravings of the audience. Which hunger is appropriate hunger? The performer not only satisfies hunger but is also obliged to refine the taste of the consumer. Thus, there are 'low' performers, who only give what the audience wants. There are 'high' performers, who also uplift the audience, making them crave not just more, but better quality. But how does the performer survive? Through payment! Patronage. Before the British introduced 'tickets' and the Americans introduced 'sponsorship', there was reward (bakshish) in exchange for a satisfactory artistic meal.

The principle of exchange, the completion of the circular loop, the two-way relationship, is also found in the rituals of yagna and puja. In yagna, the devata is invoked and given food to the chant of 'svaha' and the yajaman expects wish fulfilment to the chant of 'tathastu'. In puja, the devotee offers bhoga and expects the deity to give prasada. Likewise, on stage, the performer needs to satisfy the customer to survive. The artiste is expected to somehow survive, thrive even, despite the dissatisfaction of the audience.

12

Moksha
How Sex Became Unholy

Lately, the Catholic Church has been mired in controversy over accusations that the celibate priests are indulging in sexual activities, from affairs to rape to paedophilia. The church is being criticized for sheltering rather than reprimanding such priests.

When the Catholic Church began, 2,000 years ago, there was no privileging of celibacy. The church was a gathering of people who followed the words of Jesus Christ. Among these followers, most were householders, some noblemen, some slaves. Women, too, played a critical role. However, as Christianity became a powerful force in the Roman Empire, we find the church insisting that Christian priests and missionaries become celibate. It was a tool used to ensure the priests were more loyal to the church than to their private households, much like the eunuch culture thrived in China to ensure eunuchs, often employed in the court, were loyal to the emperor and no one else.

How the idea of celibacy entered Christianity is surrounded by a lot of discussion and debate. One of the major influences was probably the awareness of the hermit traditions of India. Even before the Roman Empire, the Greeks in Alexander's time who travelled to India had encountered the gymnosophists, naked wise men who were celibate and considered holy. They were probably Jain and Buddhist monks, or some kind of Hindu yogis.

Buddhists and Jains believed that the material world of sensual delights enchanted you through women and household responsibilities. Giving up this delusion took you towards truth and wisdom. Later, tantric schools concluded that withholding semen in the body, and using rituals to make it flow 'up the spine' rather than 'out of your body', granted magical powers. Known as 'siddhi', this allowed you to walk on water and change shape and size. Christ, who never married, was declared the Son of God, and could walk on water and change water to wine, may have been influenced by these Indian ideas.

These mystical and occult ideas, originating in the East, probably from India, captured the imagination of the Church patriarchs, leading many to believe that you can find God only when you give up the world, like Christ did. Therefore, a new order emerged of the hermits and ascetics who gave up the material world, went to the desert and became monks. Also, the idea of Christ, born of a virgin and not through a sexual act, was taken to mean that sex was sinful, and by staying away from it, one redeemed oneself from the original sin. Jesus himself did not marry.

However, the idea of sex as sinful is not found in Indian traditions, wherein gods and goddesses indulge in sexual intercourse in order to create the world and bring in happiness. Buddhism, and later Jainism, introduced the idea in India that giving up sexual life was superior. Those physically strong were heroes or vira, but those who triumphed over sensuality were mahaviras, or great heroes. Celibacy was seen as strength and sensuality as weakness. This tantric idea was later adopted by Hindu monks such as Shankaracharya, Ramanuja and Madhava.

Today, we equate celibacy with social work. The popular belief is that a person who does not have sex has transcended desire. That such a man is more concerned with the welfare of the larger public world than his personal, private, selfish welfare. These beliefs, however, are cultural assumptions, nothing else.

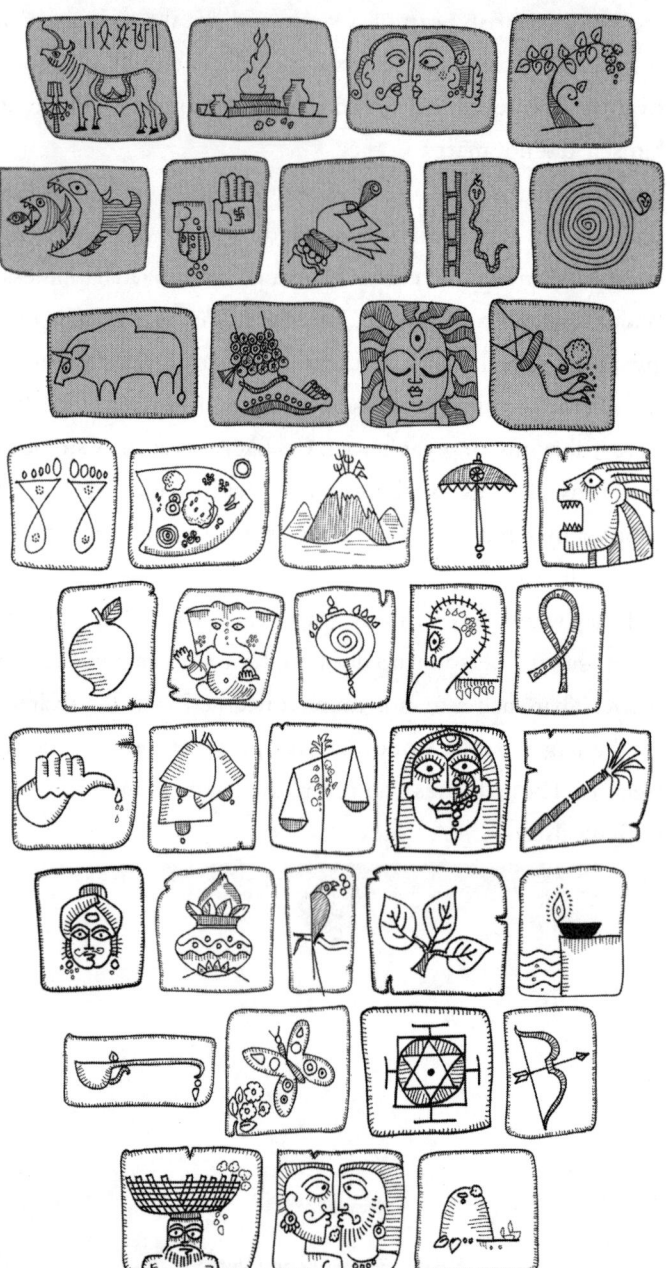

13

Dharma
Empathy Not Justice

 Once upon a time, there were two friends in a school. They were the best of friends and they promised to share everything with each other. After they graduated, one became rich and one remained poor. The poor friend went to the rich friend and asked for help. The way the friend behaved led to two endings.

In one retelling of this story, the poor friend reminded the rich friend of their childhood friendship and demanded help, in the name of their friendship. The rich friend mocked his poor friend and said that there could be no friendship between unequals, that rather than demand, the poor man ought to be begging for help and alms. This made the poor friend so angry he resolved to take revenge. The story ended in the Kurukshetra war: the poor friend is Dronacharya and the rich friend Drupada.

A similar retelling with another ending is found in the Bhagavata. Here, when the poor friend enters the rich friend's house, he comes bearing gifts. He has starved himself for three days to save the rice and gives it to his friend. Without being told, the rich friend realizes the poverty of his childhood friend and, without being asked, gives him a lot of wealth. The rich friend here is Krishna and the poor friend Sudama; it is the story of bhakti and love that we are always taught.

Clearly, these stories depict that if you don't help poor people and humiliate them, there is war and crisis in society. On the other hand, if you help poor friends and poor people, there is happiness in society. But the story is not so simplistic. We are told that Sudama starved himself for three days and gave his three portions of rice to Krishna. This is all that Sudama has done. Sudama is giving Krishna three fistfuls of rice: knowingly or unknowingly, this is his investment in a friend. Krishna reciprocates the kindness by also giving Sudama 'all that he has' in 'three measures'. We can argue that Krishna is repaying the debt resulting from receiving a gift. Unless he does so, he will be trapped in debt.

Krishna eats two fistfuls. However, just as he is about to eat the third, his wife catches hold of his hand and says, 'Leave some for us.' His wives tell him not to eat three measures but two. In essence, he could give two in reciprocity, which more than makes up for his debt, but must keep one for himself. Thus, we see prudence being brought into this story of kindness.

It was through such stories that Indians were taught about commerce, debt, exchange, reciprocity, empathy and return on investment. You give in order to get. You cannot get something without giving something. To demand something as your right, as in the case of Dronacharya, leads to rage and violence. Exchange and commerce are more egalitarian while demanding and granting rights has something feudal about it.

In Western discourse the concept of justice, including social justice, veers towards an eye for an eye, a tooth for a tooth, equal distribution of God's gifts, the influence of which can now be seen in global politics. Dharma, however, focuses less on the idea of justice and more on the idea of empathy. The strong must help the meek. Everyone has the potential to feed another. Things have to be given voluntarily, without being prodded or demanded. Great kings give of their wealth freely. This is not charity—this is investment for the future. Because hungry people are angry people who will attack and destroy what we have. Those who are fed are happy people who will collaborate.

14

Artha
Beloved of Wealth

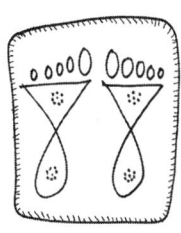 Lakshmi is the goddess of wealth. She is the most popular goddess in India. Her image can be seen in Buddhist, Jain and Hindu shrines, and at cash counters and business establishments across India. She is seen seated on a lotus, holding lotus flowers and a pot of grain, with gold coins emerging from her palm. We don't learn about her in business school though, as she is part of religion. But a study of this goddess enables us to understand how ancient Indians thought about wealth and economics.

There are many who tell me: 'actually' Lakshmi is not just about money, she is also about... This stems from the Indian discomfort with money, some of which can be (allegedly) traced to Gandhian philosophy and to monastic orders of India. We hear tales where saints fall ill when they touch money. We are told that men and women who shun money are sages, holier than the rest, and closer to God. This is extremely peculiar, considering that Lakshmi is a goddess, the beloved of Vishnu, the preserver of the world. Vishnu is popularly worshipped as Shri-nath and Tiru-pati, meaning lord of affluence and abundance.

Wisdom is all about appreciating wealth in its context, not denying wealth. As Indians, we have lost the wisdom of appreciating wealth. In the Puranas, it is said Vishnu always attracts wealth. That is why his abode, Vaikuntha, is the land of happiness; it's a playground or ranga-bhoomi. Contrast this with Swarga, the paradise of Indra, king of the devas, who is constantly fighting asuras. His abode is a rana-bhoomi or battleground, as he chases Lakshmi and tries to prevent the asuras from taking her away.

Let us not look at this as a silly children's story, or a dangerous religious concept. Let us look at this as an idea— the idea that happiness comes when Lakshmi walks our way, not when we seek to grab her. So now the question arises, is India today Swarga or Vaikuntha? We will quickly say, certainly not Swarga. But that is not true. We have many rich people and rich companies in the land who are phenomenally successful. But they are all under siege, constantly battling workers, courts, regulators; struggling to get land from villagers and licenses from the government. They are in the battlefield, like Indra.

We are constantly fighting starvation despite bumper harvests; we are Swarga. That is why Indra is not worshipped, Vishnu is. But we don't attract investments, so we are not

Vaikuntha either. That is why India is not celebrated. Investors seek Vaikuntha, where they feel their wealth will be protected and their wealth will grow. They seek Vishnu.

The fundamental difference between Indra and Vishnu is that Indra only thinks of himself and his shareholders. Indra feels entitled, like shareholders. Vishnu thinks of everyone—employees, customers, shareholders, vendors, society at large—in other words, he thinks of all the stakeholders.

A very large multinational firm recently informed me that they now think 'smart' because they want to think holistically, taking into consideration society at large in their strategic decisions, but it is tough, as the shareholders want their profit. Here we see the great struggle of Indra trying to be Vishnu. We want Vaikuntha, but we can't let go of Swarga.

15

Kama
Food of the Gods

Recently, I had the opportunity to visit both Tirupati and Varanasi. At Tirupati, the offering made to the distant and awesome Balaji (a form of Vishnu/Krishna) was food cooked in pure clarified butter. At Varanasi, I poured raw milk on the linga of Kashi Vishwanath (a form of Shiva).

I remembered the divine culinary rule my mother used to tell me whenever we went to temples—raw milk for Shiva and butter for Krishna. I have come to realize this divine culinary rule is very much the norm across India. Most Hindus, however, follow this practice mechanically. For Hinduism is an orthopraxic religion. Piety is in the doing, not in the understanding. For hundreds of years, millions of devotees have poured raw milk on Shiva's sacred image and offered butter to Krishna/Vishnu without trying to understand why.

The logic behind this is a mythical logic, based on faith, not reason, offering a window to the Hindu soul.

Shiva is an ascetic god, so withdrawn from all things worldly that he does not have a form and is represented by a formless stone (pinda, linga). Anyone, man or woman, regardless of caste, is allowed to touch his sacred image. His temples— except those in the Brahmanical superstructures of the south—are usually open-air, under banyan or pipal trees. By contrast, Vishnu participates in worldly life by taking various incarnations. As Krishna, he dances and sings and celebrates all things worldly. His temples are like palaces. He is the king, distant yet loving, reaching out to his devotees who stand for hours seeking an audience and presenting petitions.

If one thinks of milk as a metaphor for life, then raw milk is life as it comes while butter is what one can make out of life/milk. Raw milk is fit for the ascetic Shiva who does not bother to change the world. Rich, creamy butter on the other hand is for the royal Vishnu who changes the world/milk, with effort—churning, struggling, fighting, loving, enjoying. Seen through the language of symbols, the Hindu practice of offering milk to Shiva and butter to Vishnu/Krishna makes sense.

We seldom notice that blood sacrifice is offered primarily to the goddess, rarely to the male gods. It is always milk and milk products for male deities, blood for female deities. Female deities are also offered lemons and chillies, sour and pungent food. Why? The reason is, in the language of symbols, female forms represent the world around us—external reality. Male forms represent the world within us, the mind, the soul, consciousness—inner reality.

The world is everything there is—good and bad, right and wrong. In her benevolent forms, the world/goddess is associated with sugarcane and milk. In her malevolent forms the world/goddess is associated with blood and sour/bitter/pungent stuff.

Shiva and Vishnu are forms of consciousness responding to this world. The former prefers her as raw milk and accepts her soaked in blood. The latter prefers her as butter and loves and protects her so she does not cry for blood. Shiva reflects the individual who accepts life as it comes; Vishnu one who demands the best of life and is willing to work for it.

This is the language of symbols through which our ancestors are communicating their wisdom to us. You may be relishing your milk and butter, but are you listening to them?

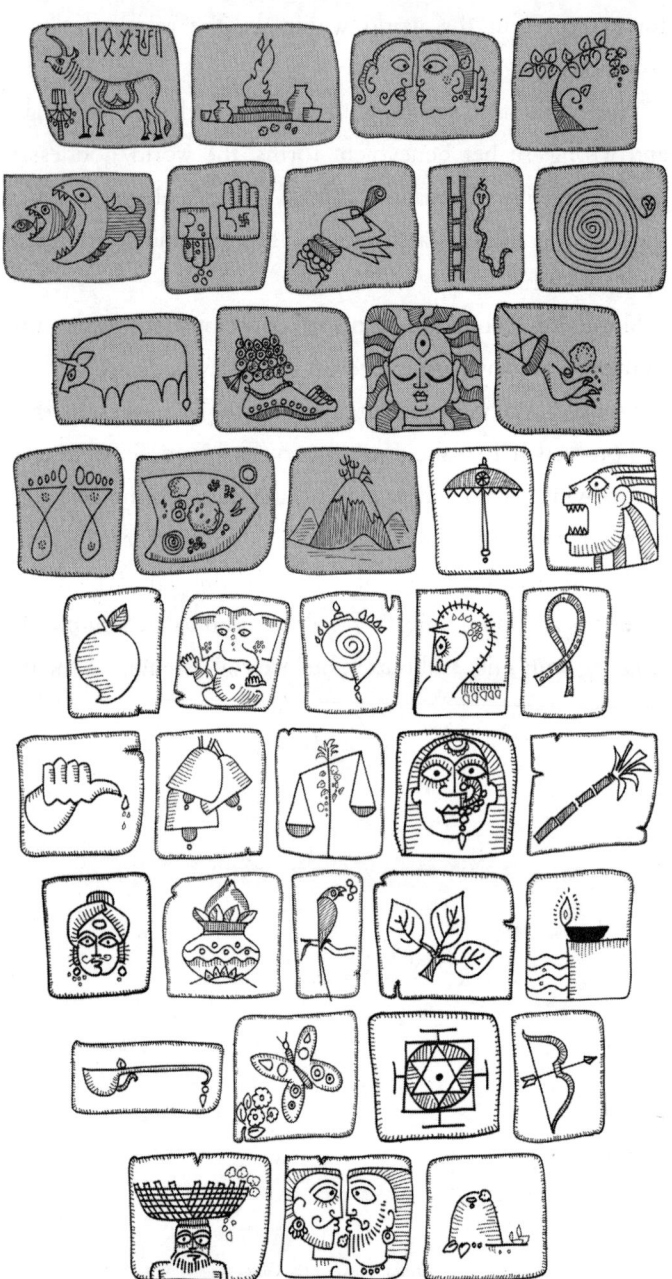

16

Moksha
Worlds Above and Below

 The Hindu cosmos or Brahmanda is visualized as a skyscraper. In the middle stands Bhu-lok, earth. Above are realms of increasing happiness, the topmost floor being Deva-lok, where all day people do nothing but enjoy the song and dance of apsaras, qualifying it to be Swarga, or paradise. Below are realms of decreasing happiness, the lowermost floor being Patala-lok, the realm of asuras, located below (tala) the feet (pa). This realm is full of gold and gems, hence the city of asuras is called Hiranyapura, city of gold.

Asuras also hold the secret of renewal and regeneration known as Sanjivani Vidya that helps plants grow. Everyone has to struggle hard to get the plants and metals necessary for sustenance from beneath the earth. Fearful that these treasures will be stolen by the residents of upper realms, the asuras are in constant guard, never able to rest or sleep or have fun, making their subterranean realm nothing short of Naraka, or hell.

After death, Hindus believe, one goes to the land of the dead, Pitr-lok, separated from the land of the living by the Vaitarni river. Here, depending on the kind of life one has led, Yama, god of death and destiny, determines the lok where one will be reborn. Good deeds grant entry into the upper happy realms, even Deva-lok if one has been really very good. Bad deeds, however, send one to the lower unhappy realms, perhaps even Patala-lok.

It must be clarified that Deva-lok is not Heaven. The latter is a concept that comes from Christian and Islamic traditions. The notion of rebirth does not exist in either Christianity or Islam: a person has only one life, and hence only one opportunity to gain entry into Heaven. That is why Christians and Muslims believe only in one Heaven (spelt in capital and singular) while Hindus entertain the ideas of multiple heavens with different grades of happiness. There are even multiple hells.

Since Hindus believe in rebirth, there are ample opportunities to enter Deva-lok, but the stay there is temporary, limited by the balance of equity of past deeds in one's karmic account. When this runs out, one has to leave Deva-lok. The good news is, stay in Patala-lok is also temporary. By doing good deeds, one can move up to a higher realm of more happiness and lesser work. Thus, a deva can become an asura and an asura can become a deva.

Dharma Artha Kama Moksha

Naturally, asuras crave access to Deva-lok while devas do everything in their power to stay there eternally. Hence, the intense yearning of the devas for the elusive Amrita, nectar of eternal youth and immortality. But while this nectar grants devas youth and immortality, it does not grant them contentment. There is always the threat of an asura attack, making devas eternally insecure and restless, preventing them from enjoying the pleasures of paradise.

This elaborate mythic geography is clearly trying to communicate a profound truth. The residents of Deva-lok have fun. The residents of Patala-lok have wealth. But neither is content. Because no amount of fun or wealth is ever enough; one always craves more.

That is why the Hindu world offers yet another destination, one that exists higher than Deva-lok, where there is no craving, only contentment. Vishnu-worshippers call this realm Vishnu-lok while Shiva-worshippers call it Shiva-lok. Unlike Deva-lok which is merely paradise, Vishnu-lok and Shiva-lok are heavens. To reach either, one has to go beyond the practice of accumulating good or bad karmas. One has to step back and appreciate life for what it is, without prejudice, without getting upset by the problems or exhilarated by the solutions. This is moksha—blissful repose born of wisdom and love.

At another level, the concept of Lok can be seen as a kind of aura or personal zone that people create around them. An energy they exude, that depends on their personality and their attitude. The Lok of some people is inviting and inclusive—we seek the company of such people. The Lok of others is repulsive—we avoid the company of such people. Thus, the whole world is full of innumerable creatures, each creating their own Lok. Scriptures suggest that by working on our attitude we can change the nature of the Lok around us—we can create Patala-lok, where we only discuss possessing things; we can create Deva-lok, where all that matters is fun; or we can create Shiva-lok or Vishnu-lok, where peace and contentment reign supreme.

17

Dharma
Buddhist Dhamma for the King

At a time when people are talking of a crisis of leadership, it makes sense to understand what kingship meant to the early Buddhists. In Buddhism, the king played a key role in preventing anarchy, establishing order and spreading the Buddhist message and way of life. A great king in Buddhist literature was known as chakravarti. The chakra represents the empire: the circumference of the wheel represents the boundaries and the spokes represent the highways that connect the capital city to the frontiers. The chakravarti possessed seven great treasures: the great wheel of kingship (a symbolic representation of power), a horse, an elephant, the queen, a commander or minister, a treasury, and landholding householders whom he protected.

Some of the earliest ideas of what a king should be come

to us from the Jataka tales: stories that speak of Buddha's previous lives, long before the one in which he attained nirvana. In many of these lives he was a king, explaining what the Buddhist idea of kingship entails.

In the Dummedha Jataka, we learn that a king should be stern: like the king of Benaras, who threatens his subjects with beheading and impaling if they do not follow the righteous path. In fear, everybody lives righteously, performing their roles in society and being generous with wise men and strangers. Thus, this king uses the threat of violence to create a good society.

In the Brahmadatta Jataka, we learn of a compassionate king who saves three eggs in the nest of a bird he has accidentally shot and killed. He takes care of the eggs as a parent would. Three birds emerge from the eggs: an owl, a myna (starling) and a parrot. They end up giving the king wise counsel which helps him become a great king. Thus, it is important for a king to be compassionate.

In the Makhadeva Jataka, we meet a wise king who knows that everything passes away. When he finds a single grey hair on his head, he realizes it is time to retire and he bequeaths his kingdom to his children. We also learn of the generous king, Shibhi. When Indra, taking the form of a Brahmin, asks Shibhi for his left eye, Shibhi, without hesitation, cuts it out and gives it to him. With his right eye, Shibhi observes the happiness on the Brahmin's face and offers him that eye, too. Thus, generosity is revealed as a quality of kingship.

We also learn of a quality which a king should not have:

greed. We hear of a great king, Mandhatta, who ruled a vast kingdom for eighty-four thousand years. He was so great a king that neighbouring kings renounced their thrones and asked him to rule in their stead. However, he felt dissatisfied, feeling he should rule an even larger empire. So, he rose to a heaven above earth and ruled there for another long period. In time, he began to wish to rule the heaven of the thirty-three gods.

When he went there, Indra gave him half the heaven and ruled the other half himself. As time passed, Mandhatta again experienced discontent. He now desired to rule all of heaven itself. He planned to overthrow Indra and become king. In the past his greatness had inspired people to voluntarily give up their kingdoms and make him king of a greater land. However, this time, rather than wait and let it come to him voluntarily, he tried to grab power. Consequently, he not only lost his divine glory but his place in heaven and slipped down to earth and died. This is a cautionary tale against over-ambition: a lesson that we seem to never learn even in modern times.

In the Buddhist scheme of things, it is the duty of the king not only to spread dhamma amongst his people, but also to protect the dharma teachings when the world turns corrupt and people become incapable of following the Buddha's way. That is why Buddhist kings, like Ashoka, 2,300 years ago, and Kanishka, 1,900 years ago, played a key role in gathering Buddhist knowledge and codifying it. Buddhist lore constantly spoke of how Buddhism would end because of attacks by invaders and because of infighting amongst various Buddhist teachers. But as long as there was a good king, the teachings of the Buddha would survive.

The king, or leader, in the Buddhist scheme of things was thus not just a politician but a guardian of morality and ethics. He had to be not just brave but also compassionate and understanding towards his people. He had to understand the fragility of his reign and the dangers of over-ambition. And most importantly, he had to secure what he knew would eventually fade away, so that what died in the present would be revived in the future. The Buddhist king was thus not just seen in materialistic terms but also in the deepest spiritual terms.

18

Artha
Hindu Aspiration

 Many people say that India's caste system is simply a rational division of labour to promote efficiency and effectiveness. Those who say this usually associate themselves with the top two tiers (Brahmin and Kshatriya), less commonly with the third tier (Vaishya), and hardly ever with the fourth tier (Shudra). We hear people say 'I am proud to be a Brahmin/Kshatriya/Vaishya' but not many say 'I am proud to be a Shudra'. Clearly some tiers are deemed glamorous and more aspirational than others, despite all talk of equality.

The chatur-varna or four-fold system was the hallmark of Vedic society. But it is completely theoretical, probably based on 'aptitude' rather than 'birth'; though one is not entirely sure. The four tiers were: transmitters of Vedic lore (Brahmins), those who controlled the land (Kshatriyas), those who controlled the markets (Vaishyas), and the service-providers (Shudras).

In practice, Indian society has long been divided into jatis. There are thousands of jatis, as against four varnas. When people say caste, they are referring to a European term used to explain jati, not varna. We often confuse the two. Jati was an economic-political unit, based on vocation. You inherited your jati from your father. Jati was established by a relatively simple idea called 'roti-beti': you ate with members of your own jati, and you married a boy or girl from your own jati. A jati functioned like a tribe. Just as inter-tribe marriage was not permitted, inter-jati marriage was not permitted. Crossing jati lines could lead to violence.

The relative position of a jati in a village hierarchy was determined by regional power play. For example, the jati of Kayasthas in the Gangetic plains emerged with the rise of Hindu bureaucrats in Mughal courts. Not many people in south India would know how to locate a Kayastha in their community. Likewise, few in Rajasthan would understand who the Lingayats of Karnataka were, and where they stood in the caste hierarchy.

As a rule of thumb, those involved in priestly matters were Brahmins, and those who controlled the land were Kshatriyas. But where did you locate the bureaucrat who served in the king's court? Was he Brahmin or Kshatriya or simply a Shudra, a service-provider? New warlords who came from outside like the Sakas and Pallavas and settled in India were anointed as Kshatriyas and linked to the gods and to Puranic kings to grant them legitimacy. A rich moneylender was a Vaishya, but was he not a service-provider, providing banking services? And was a mercenary, who owned no land, and sold his military services to the highest bidder, a Kshatriya or a Shudra?

Mapping the thousands of jatis to the four varnas has always been a challenge. In the south, Brahmins became powerful by controlling many farmlands—the Brahmadeya villages and Agraharas. But did that not make them landowners and hence Kshatriyas? Were the Peshwas of Maharashtra to be considered Brahmins or Kshatriyas or administration service-providers? These were complex matters. They led to quarrels.

The Vedas do speak of a diverse society. The dominant members of society—the Brahmins, the landowners, the rich and the powerful—turned this concept of diversity into a hierarchical society. They did it using the Dharmashastras. In the Dharmashastras, including the Manusmriti, the Brahmin jatis mapped themselves to Brahmin varna. They were not interested in mapping the thousands of other jatis.

There was hierarchy amongst the Brahmin jatis. The ones who chanted Vedic lore saw themselves as superior to those who worked as purohits in temples. Those who officiated in marriages were seen as superior to those who conducted funerals. Likewise, there was hierarchy amongst Shudras. Those who provided services like barbers were superior to those who worked as manual scavengers. This hierarchy did not come from any scripture; it came from regional politics.

Every society in the world has economic and political

hierarchies. What makes the jati system unique is the hierarchy of purity. Some service-providers were deemed 'dirty' and denied access to the village well and stripped of all human dignity. This is the worst aspect of the caste system, something that is often denied by apologists. Was this recommended by the Vedas? No, it was not. The Vedas speak of atma, the soul, that is eternally pure, and values diversity not hierarchy. They speak of fear and ignorance that nourishes the aham, the ego, which values the body, wealth and power, and institutes various hierarchies.

Until the Industrial Revolution, every society was controlled by the intellectual elite (priests and philosophers), the landed gentry and the mercantile class. The rest were serfs and slaves. Craftsmen and traders had lower status. Lower still were the labourers. The Industrial Revolution created a new class of bankers and businessmen and factory workers and clerks and corporate executives. Social mobility became a possibility. Still, society was dominated by the educated (Brahmins) and the powerful (Kshatriyas) and the rich (Vaishyas), not the service-providers (Shudras), which is a politically correct word for servant. It is so in India; it is so elsewhere.

We do not mind being servants (dasa) of god or guru, but not of other people because of an innate feudal mindset. And we fear equality because it strips us of identity and status, and dissolves us in a homogenous social soul. Like the Brahmins of yore (and the British, and the government) we continue to map ourselves on the theoretical and simplistic four-layered society of the Vedas, more often than not to feel good about ourselves. When power is factored in some divisions of labour become aspirational and superior, and others less desired, and inferior.

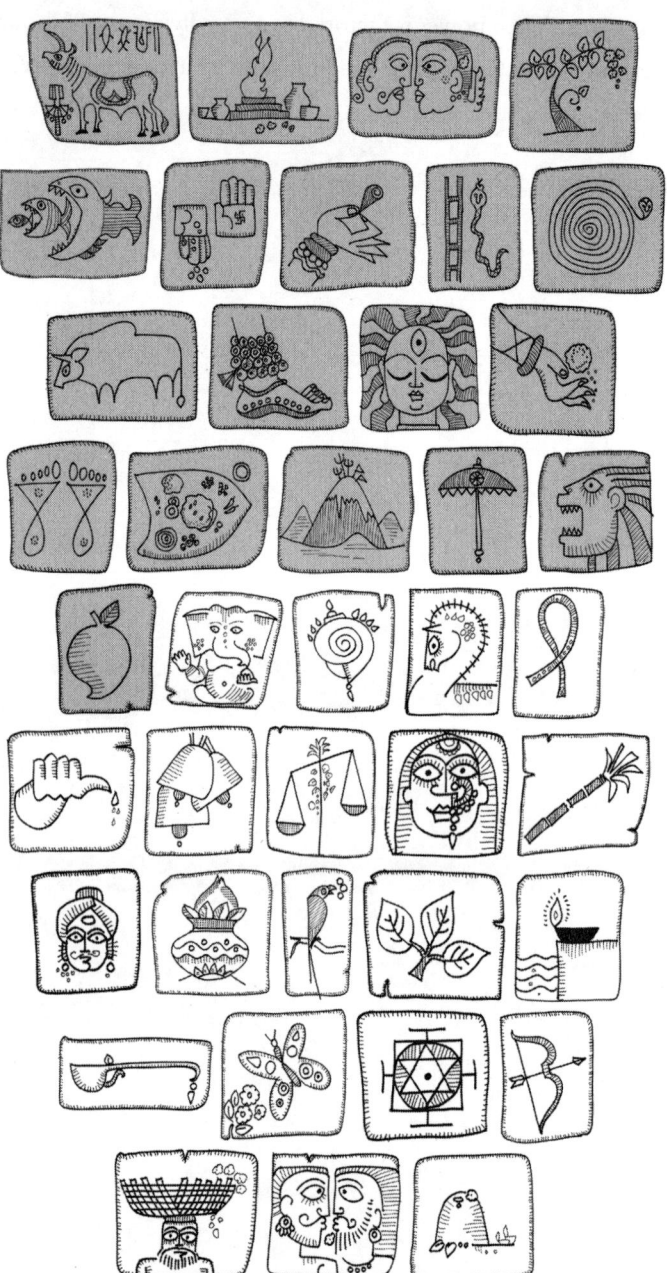

19

Kama
The Vessel of Rasa

 Typically, in India, we refer to an actor in a play or a character in a book as 'patra', which literally means vessel. Why? To understand this, we perhaps have to appreciate the two distinct ways of telling a story: the Western way and the Indian way.

Aristotle, the Greek philosopher, student of Plato, teacher of Alexander, is considered the fountainhead of the Western approach to narratives. His *Poetics* looks at narratives very intellectually, focusing on one character, the hero, and his transformation following a dramatic event. Here, storytelling begins by paying attention to the idea, which is expressed through plot and character. The audience watches this, identifies with the character, and experiences catharsis, a purging of their own bottled-up emotions. Thus, the journey is from the head to the heart.

Bharata composed the *Natyashastra* probably around the same time as Aristotle. He, too, was interested in theatre as a medium. However, there is a fundamental difference between Aristotle's *Poetics* and Bharata's *Natyashastra*. Bharata focuses more on the sensations (rasa) evoked in the audience, and the emotions (bhava) of the performer, and less on the story itself. The expressions, posture and gestures of the performer need to be rooted in a particular emotion (bhava) so that it evokes an aesthetic sensory experience (rasa) in the audience. Here, the journey is from the heart to the head.

The Western way of storytelling focuses on one character, one plot, one transformation, and one dominant emotion. In complex storytelling, multiple linear storylines are woven together into a tapestry. Here, the idea matters and through the idea one emotion rises and falls. We see this in Shakespeare's plays: the hesitation of *Hamlet*, the romance of *Romeo and Juliet*, the impatient passion of *Othello*. Each of these plays has a clear story, with a distinct emotion.

By contrast, in the Indian way of storytelling the point is to nourish the audience with a whole range of sensations and emotions. At the end of the story, has the viewer experienced happiness, anger, pleasure, hatred, love, compassion, sorrow? Here, the idea does not matter as much. When we think of Ram or Krishna or Shiva, an emotion is evoked, and the whole purpose of their sagas is to reinforce that emotion. As in an Indian thali, where there are different flavours, the rasa associated with Ram becomes distinct and gets amplified because of other rasas evoked by other characters of the Ramayana such as Lakshman, Sita, Hanuman and Ravana.

Hollywood films, not surprisingly, are famous for great plots and characters. Bollywood films, by contrast, are known more for their songs, dances, the colours, operatic style, melodrama, where plot and character are sometimes afterthoughts. In a Hollywood film, what matters is the pace and build-up to the climax. In a Bollywood film, what matters is the rush of sensations and emotions, so there is no discomfort with disjointed stories or irrational plots. In Western storytelling the actor is the container of an idea. In Indian storytelling, the actor is the vessel that nourishes the audience with rasa.

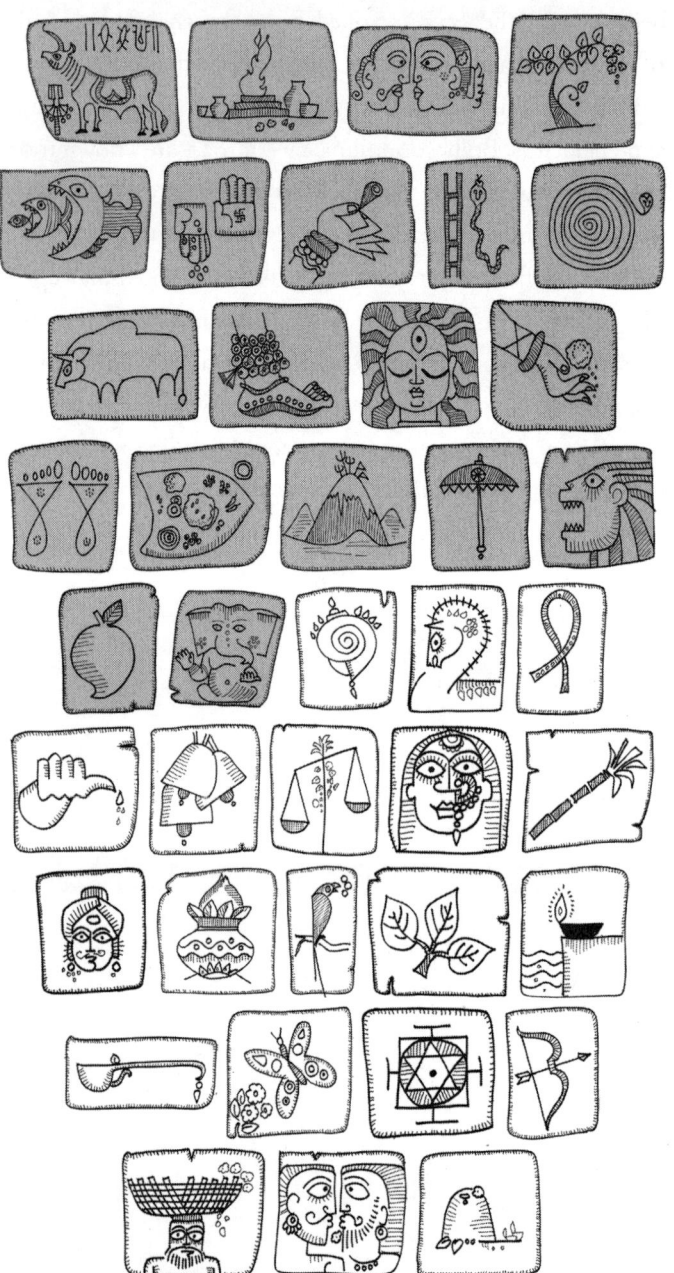

20

Moksha
My World and The World

One day, the two brothers Ganesha and Kartikeya decided to race three times around the world. Kartikeya, being more athletic, jumped on his peacock and flew around the oceans, the continents and the stars. The elephant-headed Ganesha simply went around his parents, and declared himself the winner. When asked for an explanation, Ganesha said, 'I went around my world. You went around the world. Which matters more?'

'The world' is objective; truth independent of human imagination. 'My world' is subjective; truth dependent on human imagination. Different people of the world imagine the world differently.

The ancient Greeks believed you live only once. And the one who does something extraordinary in this life, earns a place in Elysium, the heaven of heroes. In the Greek world, the gods of Olympus were capricious; they sought to keep humans in check lest they rose up in revolt. They feared being overthrown by humans, just as they had overthrown the Titans and the Titans had overthrown the Giants before them.

Heroes were men who did extraordinary things despite the odds thrown in their direction by the Fates who, in turn, were controlled by the gods. Greek epics spoke of fathers who tried to kill their newborn sons who were prophesized to kill them, and of sons who rose up against father and god and authority, fought the monsters created by them, and after many an adventure, achieved the impossible to become heroes worthy of adoration. Glory lay in defiance of authority and transgression of rules. This is the recurrent theme in the stories of Hercules, Theseus, Jason and Achilles.

The Abrahamic faiths (Judaism, Christianity, Islam) also speak of one life, followed by an afterlife. But the world imagined by them is very different from the one of the ancient Greeks. The Biblical world referred to a kind and loving God who cared for his Creation and whose children kept breaking the rules he asked them to follow. So, we have the story of the transgression of Adam and Eve, and of various prophets like Moses, kings like David, who struggle to uphold the commandments of God, and make others follow them in faith. Glory here lay in obedience and compliance; it gets you not to the Elysium of the heroes but to what the Quran refers to as Jannat for the faithful.

Who is right? Should life be about defiance or compliance,

about breaking rules or following rules? If the question was posed to a rishi from India, he would ask: why should the answer be this or that, why can the answer not be this *and* that? He would say both are okay, depending on the context. So Hindu mythology has both Krishna who breaks rules and Ram who follows them. Krishna belongs to Dvapara Yuga and Ram belongs to Treta Yuga. But are not Krishna and Ram two different characters? Not at all, the rishi would say; they were two lifetimes of Vishnu, who is God.

The rishi believed in rebirth. He believed we do not live just one life; we live infinite lives, one life after another, again and again. Death is not a full stop; it is a comma. And so, you have the option of living one life in defiance and one life in compliance, depending on whether the father, or authority, or deity, of that life is cruel (like Olympian gods) or caring (like the God of Abraham). This view is shared by most religions of Indian origin, including Jainism and Buddhism.

Refusal to acknowledge these imagined realities, these 'my' worlds, is the root cause of cultural intolerance, human insensitivity and the clash of civilizations. It happened once nearly 2,300 years ago on the banks of the River Indus. There, Alexander the Great, after having conquered Persia, found what he called a gymnosophist or a naked wise man. He was perhaps a Jain muni or perhaps a yogi, who sat on a rock and meditated all day and gazed at the stars all night. 'What are you doing?' asked Alexander. 'Experiencing nothingness,' answered the gymnosophist. Then the gymnosophist asked, 'What are you doing?' Alexander replied, 'I am conquering the world.' Both chuckled and parted ways, each one thinking the other a fool.

For Alexander, the denominator of life was only one; so, the value of his existence was the sum total of his achievements. Therefore, conquering the world was important to him. For the gymnosophist, the denominator of life was infinity; so the value of his existence—no matter what he did—was zero. So, reflecting on the world and seeking its meaning by 'experiencing nothingness' was important to him. Then who is right: Alexander or the gymnosophist? What is right: one life or rebirth? Intolerance stems from valuing one imagined reality over the other.

Significantly, science—in its quest for the objective truth— aligns itself with one-life subjective truths. But which one? Greek or Abrahamic? Alexander's subjective truth works for those who want to conquer the world. But there are many who are not interested.

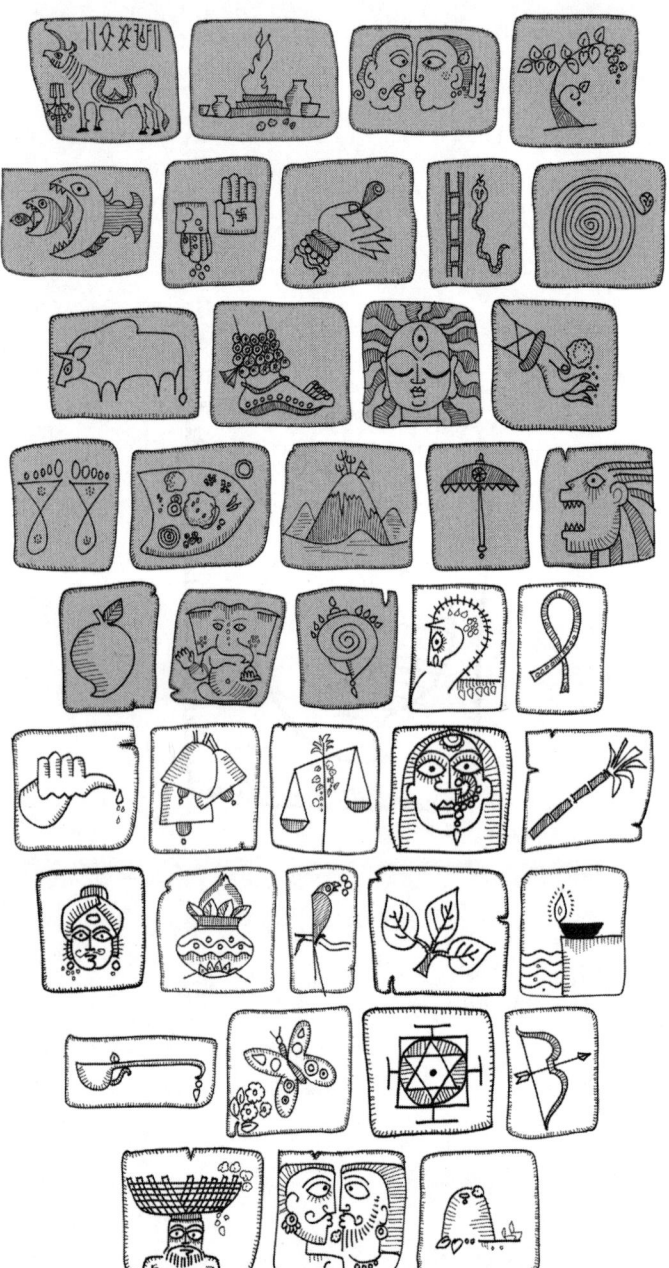

21

Dharma
Dharma Is Not a
Game of Thrones

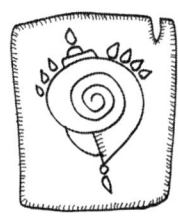

King Nriga was cursed to be a lizard because he, without realizing it, had stolen from one of his subjects. Nriga was known for donating cows to the sages of his kingdom. One of the donated cows slipped out of her master's cowshed and returned to the royal cowshed. Since the royal cowshed had thousands of cows, none of the royal servants noticed her return. Nriga then gave the same cow to another sage. When this sage was returning to his hermitage with Nriga's gift, the first sage recognized his cow, claimed ownership over her, and accused the second sage of theft. When the second sage clarified that he had received the cow from King Nriga himself, the first sage accused the king of theft.

'That cow was given to me. She is mine. Not the king's. How then can the king gift her to another? This means the king stole my cow and gave the stolen cow to another sage. I accuse the king of stealing from his own subjects.' Investigations revealed what had happened. Nriga apologized to the first sage and offered to compensate him with a hundred cows. The sage refused. He wanted his cow back. Nriga then went to the second sage and offered to compensate him with a hundred cows. But the second sage refused to return his gift. For this act of hurting his subjects, albeit committed unintentionally, and quite accidentally, Nriga was cursed to turn into a lizard, and stay in this form until he met Krishna. Nriga accepted his punishment with grace.

This story is told by Bhisma to the Pandavas in the Anushasana Parva of the Mahabharata as he gives them lessons on raj-dharma, or what makes a great king. A king is responsible for the happiness of his subjects. He is responsible for all the hurt he causes them, even without meaning to. This story is significant as Nriga is an ancestor of Ram, and from the much venerated Ikshavaku clan of the solar dynasty, which gave birth to many great kings, including several Jain Tirthankaras.

We live in times where politicians talk of Ram and Ram-rajya, but take no lessons on what raj-dharma meant to Ram and his Ikshavaku clan. They refuse to take responsibility for the failures of their own governance. Quite unlike Ram, who, as per one oral narrative, despite being from the solar dynasty, called himself Ram-chandra, eclipsing his name with the moon to acknowledge his unfair treatment of his innocent wife, Sita, who had been banished to protect the royal reputation from public gossip.

We are told that the legendary king Vikramaditya, renowned for his bravery, generosity and governance, also belonged to the solar dynasty. Many years after Vikramaditya's reign, Bhoja wanted to sit on his famous throne, which had been discovered in the fields around his ancient kingdom. But when he was about to sit on this throne, the statues of the thirty-two yoginis that formed the base of the throne asked Bhoja if he had thirty-two qualities that made him as good a king as Vikramaditya had been. Bhoja cultivated these thirty-two qualities and only then sat on the legendary king's throne. We live in times when no noble quality is required to be a king. Kingship is based on votes, and votes are won through emotional rhetoric, fanciful storytelling and false promises. More Natya-shastra and less Dharma-shastra.

Who do people turn to today, when kings are busy fighting enemies, real and imagined, or blaming corrupt kings of yore for all governance failures, and when tongues of even well-meaning vidushakas (court jesters who were also critics) are swiftly severed?

In the jungle, the strong feed on the weak. This is matsya nyaya (law of fishes), acceptable for animals, not humans. When humans behave so, it is adharma. In human culture, the strong have to take care of the weak. As per the Manusmriti, gods created kings to establish dharma: to create an ecosystem where the weak can also thrive. In raj-dharma, the kingdom is more important than the throne. In raj-niti, it is only a game of thrones; people don't matter except for votes and taxes. Today raj-dharma is seen as idealistic and raj-niti (politics) is seen as more realistic.

For all the talk of Hindu revival, politicians refuse to accept this definition of raj-dharma, insisting that the 'system' is the problem, as the 'system' is designed for the strong. And so, they spend time in raj-niti, helping the rich, who in exchange help political parties accumulate funds secretly, so that politicians can sit on the throne, enjoying power without any responsibility or accountability, letting roads rot and bridges collapse, knowing there is always someone else to blame. If today's politicians lived in Nriga's time, they would change the media narrative and declare the sages to be thieves and claim the cows for themselves.

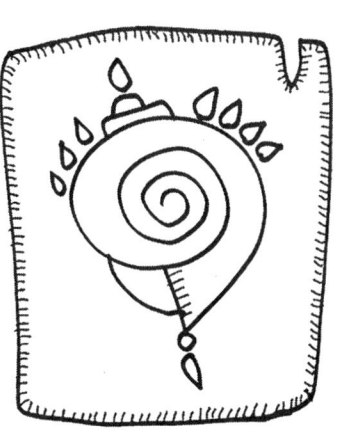

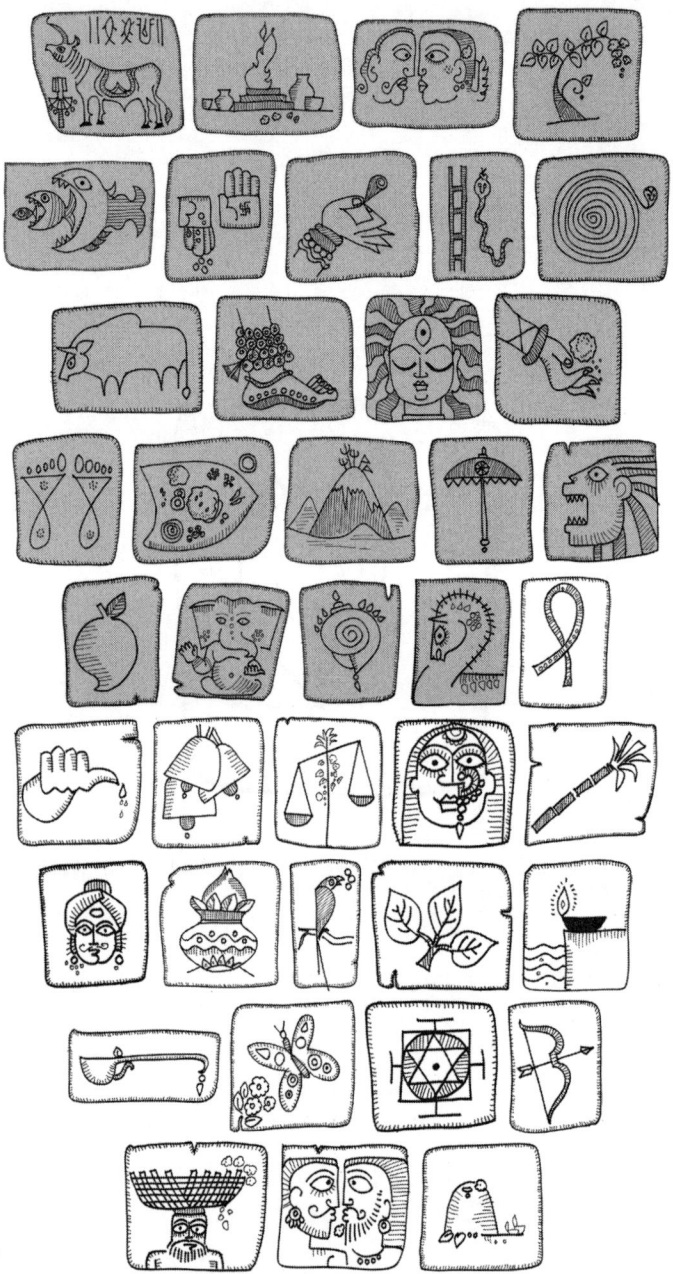

22

Artha
Feudalism and Economy

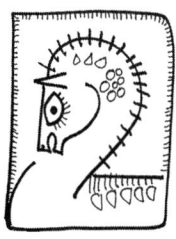 In Hindi, the word 'bazaru' is an insult. Translated as 'of the market', it does not sound so bad. Translated as 'peddler', it captures the derision of feudal society for the market.

Feudal societies are typically agrarian and land (kshetra) based and so controlled by the land-owning gentry (Kshatriyas), often confused with warriors who once guarded cattle and farmlands, and later realized they could outsource farming and herding to peasants, serfs and tenants, while retaining rights as owners. The market (bazaar) was the domain of the manufacturing craftsmen, until the middlemen—traders and moneylenders (Vaishyas, Vaniks)—took their place and pushed the goods-producing artisan lower in the social hierarchy, a notch above the service-providers (Shudras).

The discomfort with all things associated with the market can be seen in India when holy men warn people not to be bhogis (those who seek satisfaction of desires), when the desire for goods and services and ideas is what creates the market, with the goods provided by the craftsmen, the service by the Shudras, and the ideas by the Brahmins. Rather than ask for fair wages (dakshina) one was encouraged to do service (seva) without expectations (nishkama).

This feudal tone is evident in the general disdain in India for servants (chakars) and slaves (dasa) who are shoved to the bottom of the caste pyramid. In popular religion, to provide free service to God, or his middleman, the guru, is a sign of deep piety. The concubine, loyal to a single feudal patron, was granted more respect than the prostitute who auctioned her services but was a thorough professional, treating all paying customers equally.

Feudal, land-based economies of Kshatriyas value Lakshmi as Bhu-devi (tangible land) while market-based economies of Vaishyas value Lakshmi as Shree-devi (intangible value). These two economies vie for power to dominate society. In art, the former is represented as a pot of grain, the latter by a pot of gold.

The battle between the Old World of Europe and the New World of America is a battle between Kshatriyas (old class of landowners) and Vaniks (new class of emerging industrialists and bankers). So, they split from the old church (Catholic), and created their own new church (Protestant), that did not look down on moneylending, and moved from Europe to America to create a republic that supported free enterprise and did not care much for inherited entitlement. In the new world order created by Americans, professionalism matters more than loyalty, the fickle Shree-devi who needs to be wooed is preferred over Bhu-devi who has to be conquered and controlled.

In India, the feudal orders were legitimized by Brahmins, who helped establish new villages, especially in the south, and created systems for tax collection for God's first servant, the king. The market forces were patronized by the monastic Buddhist and Jain orders, who looked down on violence that was integral to war and agricultural activities. Not surprisingly, holy Hindu texts such as the Ramayana and Mahabharata revolved around Kshatriyas and Brahmins, while the Buddhist Jatakas revolved around merchants and traders.

Of course, things were not always so simple. There were many kings who favoured Buddhism and Jainism; in Southeast Asia, for instance, it is Buddhism that prevailed over Brahminism. At the same time, there were many trading communities that embraced Brahminism, such as the Gujarati Vaishnavas and the Tamil Chettiars.

Overall, however, India favoured Kshatriya feudalism to the market-based economies of Vaishyas. Once a country of sea-faring merchants, we outsourced international trade to Arabs, and became inward-looking, frogs in the well (kupa-manduka), valuing submission to authority (bhakti) rather than revelling in the quest for bhoga in the bazaar.

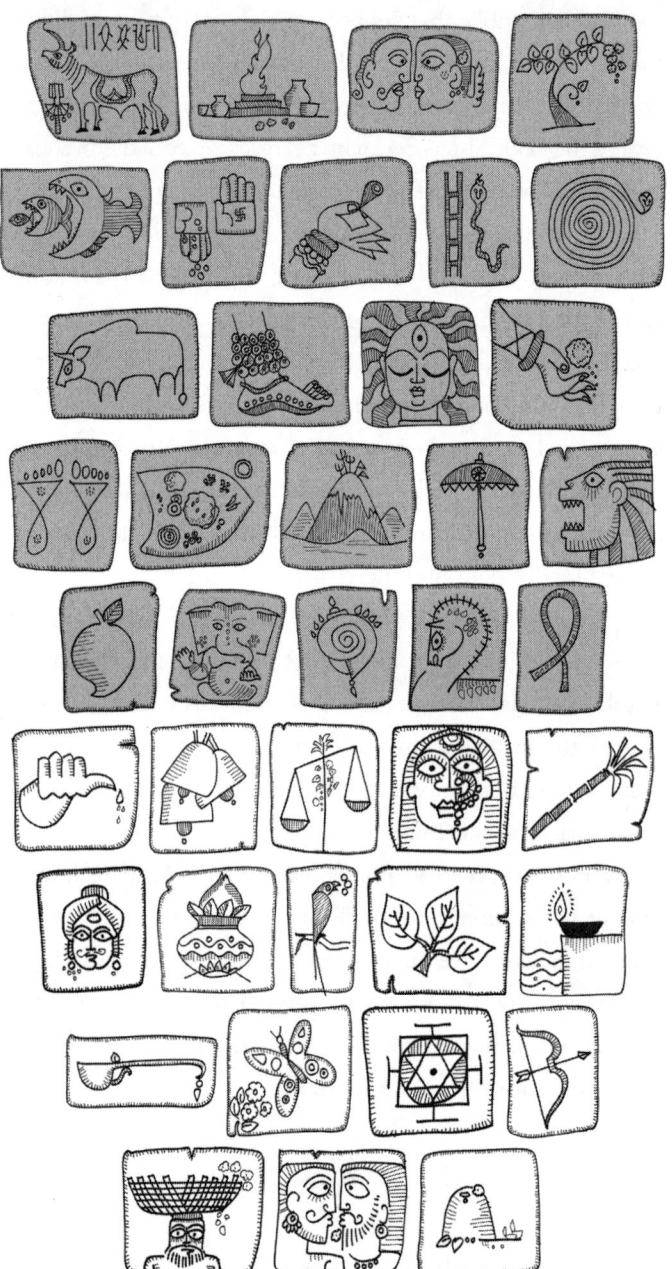

23

Kama
Desire's Bow and Destiny's Noose

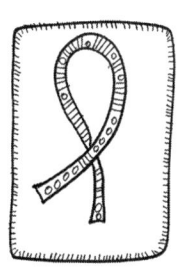

Elections are a time to express desire, while the years in between are a time to face our destiny. For the arrow of our desire creates the noose of our destiny. In Hindu mythology, desire and destiny are the two principles governing all life. Desire propels action; action creates reaction; and reaction creates the circumstances we experience from which we cannot escape. In other words, desire eventually creates destiny.

Desire emerges with the transformation of a non-living object into a living organism that experiences hunger, thirst, yearning and longing. If there was no hunger or thirst, there would be no life. Kamadeva, the god of love, is associated with a bow made of sugar cane, whose bowstring is made of bees and butterflies and the arrows tipped with flowers.

The bow symbolizes a weapon that fills the body with longing. When struck by Kama's five arrows, we come alive with desire, we yearn for food, satisfaction, pleasure and survival.

In the ascetic traditions of India, including Buddhism, Jainism and Hinduism, the monks believed desire was the cause of all suffering. Desire became adverse. Therefore, the purpose of life became outgrowing it.

In mythology, Shiva opens his third eye and sets aflame the god of love and turns him into a heap of ash. However, the Goddess confronts Shiva and demands that he resurrect the love god: because, without Kamadeva, nature cannot function. Shiva realizes the dangers of curbing desire and Kama is resurrected in the form of a goddess called Kamakshi (or Kamini), the one who evokes desire. Shiva, from being Kamantaka (destroyer of desire), turns into Kameshwara (master of desire).

If desire is represented by events over which we have no control, destiny is represented by the pasa or noose that binds us to experience the destiny created by our own desires. This is karma. People popularly confuse karma with fatalism. However, as we have seen, that is an incomplete understanding of karma. Karma is both: actions we do voluntarily and actions we perform involuntarily. This is conceptualized as the noose of Yama.

Yama is the god of death and rebirth. He maintains the record of all our actions: the debts we incur in our life (through desire) which we must repay in a future life. The noose of Yama is really the noose of debt that binds us to the cycle of birth and rebirth. Only when we repay our debts are we liberated from the noose and we attain what is called moksha or mukti: freedom from hunger, fear, attachment and the circle of life and death. When one is dying, Yama hurls the noose and pulls the life-breath out of the body. He keeps one tied to this noose until one repays one's debts, which is essentially the reactions of past actions. These reactions create either good or bad contexts in our life, which we are obliged to endure in our future lives.

Kama's bow and arrow hold the potential of the choice of actions, what we choose in response to the destiny we encounter. Yama's noose embodies what fate has in store for us. For instance, the arrows we shoot in the election booth will determine the noose that will follow.

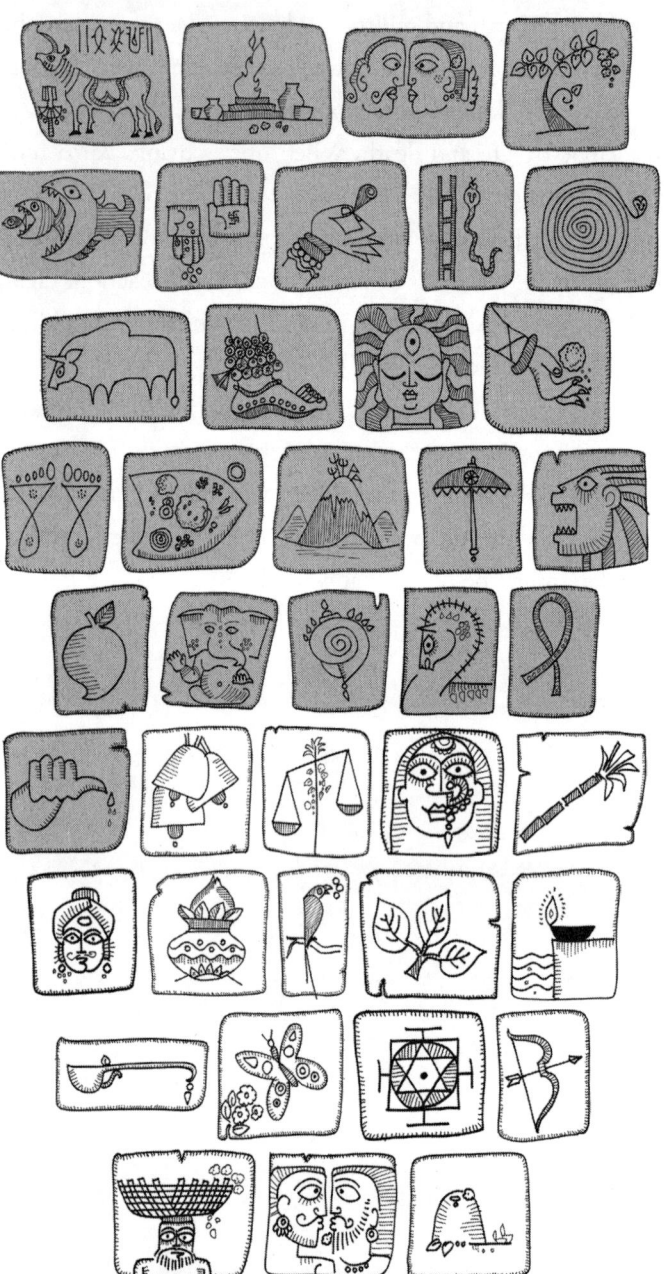

24

Moksha
Our Expiry Date

Everything in nature has an expiry date. Even the sun. Talk to an astrophysicist and they will tell you when the sun will eventually die. Nothing lasts forever. We know that. And yet, the culture around us is all about 'built to last'. The obsession with defying mortality, defying nature, being immortal is at the heart of human madness. It is what destroys society and ideology and relationships.

The richest man in the world, the most powerful technocrats of the world, are all eventually going to die, even if they are being advised by the best dieticians and gym trainers and doctors. Have they imagined a world after them? Do they imagine a world where they are not remembered at all? Do they accept that the world does not really need them? Are they okay with invalidation? Not if you follow American schools of management, where it is all about having a dream, a purpose, and leaving behind a legacy.

For all our scientific temper, and despite historical evidence that some of the greatest empires in the world have collapsed, that emperors have been forgotten, that scientists and their great inventions are no longer meaningful, management gurus still harp on the fiction of immortality and permanence—because they serve the mortal man's anxiety, rather than help us transcend it.

Death, or the concept of an expiry date, is at the heart of spirituality. Death makes us question the meaning of life and makes seekers out of us. We turn to holy books and holy men, to gods and prophets, we value ambition and achievement and success. Death makes us anxious. Take away death, usher in immortality, and why would stress exist? For a world without death would be a world without change, without time, without memory or its loss.

It is man's obsession with death and therefore questions of immortality that have shaped the religions of the world. In Abrahamic religions, the solution offered is not to think, just follow the rules, and trust God, who is permanent. In Karmic religions, the monks speak of transcending death through introspection and meditation, or surviving through children and family name. The ancient Greeks and Romans genuinely believed that achievements ensured one's immortality; the bards sang of preserving your legacy forever. And this Greco-Roman 'pagan' thought is at the heart of the American dream—the desire to be a hero who does the impossible despite odds and opposition. It's the classic rags-to-riches story in Hollywood.

In Hinduism, the concept of an expiry date was acknowledged through the notion of ashrama-dharma. Everyone speaks of varna-dharma or India's ubiquitous caste system, but they seem to have forgotten the other half of this system: one that acknowledged the expiry date of your caste, as well as your life.

After training (brahmacharya or student stage), every man was supposed to do his duties and enjoy caste privileges (grihastha or householder stage) only till his grandson was born. Then he had to teach his grandchildren his skills (vanaprastha or retired stage). When the grandchildren had children of their own, he had to renounce the world (sanyasa or hermit stage); free of caste duties and shorn of caste privileges, ready to accept death, having supported life.

In modern corporate management, it translates into the talent pipeline—not just aspiring to be a CEO (phase 1), or being a CEO (phase 2), but preparing the next CEO (phase 3) and then living without the glamour of the CEO life (phase 4), knowing that every position is temporary, hence a seductive delusion, like life itself. But to let go of a powerful corporate role is tough.

Once we have tasted fame and power it is difficult to let go. And so to stay relevant even after retirement, government servants, even judges, it is whispered, become more corrupt as their end of term approaches.

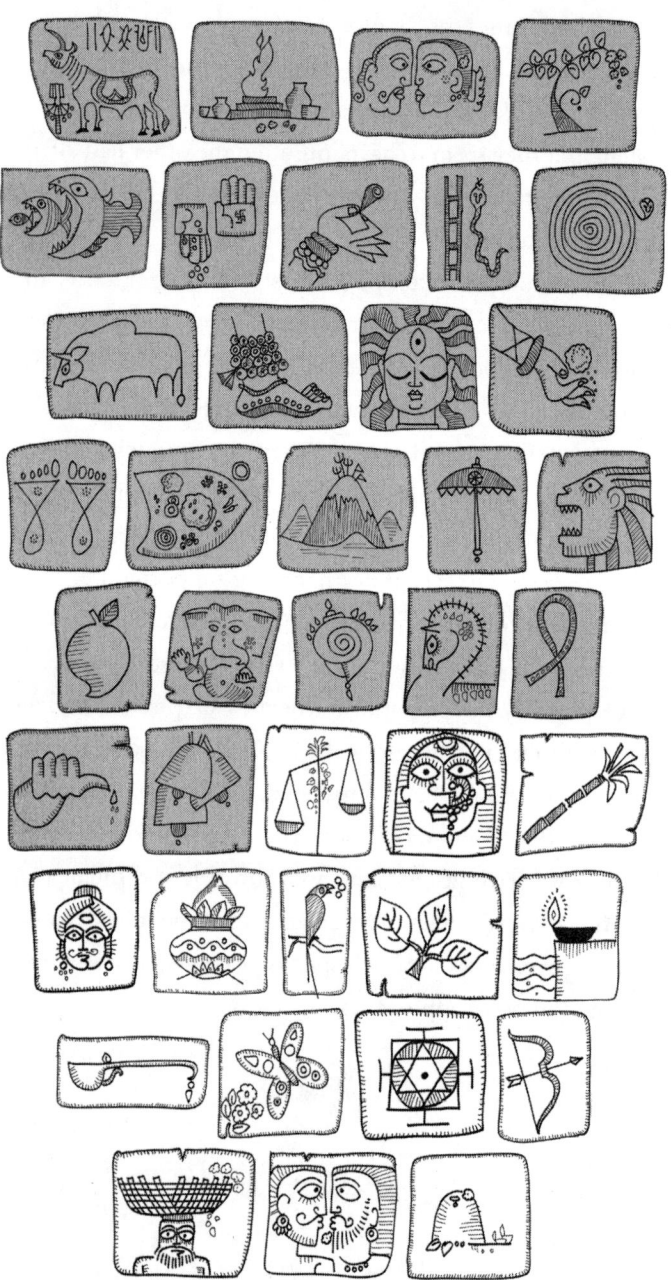

25

Dharma
Emergency Dharma

As we go through a global pandemic, which has demanded a major change in our lifestyle and which will have a long-lasting impact on the economy, it is a good time to remember a conversation in the Mahabharata, where Bhishma tells the Pandavas about Apaddharma, or dharma during crisis.

In the Shatapatha Brahmana, dharma is defined as a state of being that reverses jungle law. In the jungle, might is right; but, in a civilized society, the mighty take care of the weak. In the Dharma-shastras, this principle is operationalized using the varna-ashrama guidelines.

Varna means respecting and following the vocation of our forefathers. The various vocations are classified into four groups: the knowledge economy of Brahmins; the land economy of

Kshatriyas; the market economy of Vaishyas and the service economy of Shudras. Ashrama means being a student for the first quarter of life; a householder in the second; a retired person in the third (when grandchildren are born); and renunciation in the fourth (when the grandchildren are married). This is the complete division of labour as per Varna dharma. There is no burden of more than two generations on the earth's resources based on our life cycle. This conceptual framework applies in an ideal situation; but how does one work during crises? Apaddharma talks about functioning during a crisis.

Once, when there was a drought, Vishwamitra had nothing to eat, and was forced to eat the meat of a dog. Another crisis could be when a husband died without having children. In such a scenario, the Dharma-shastras allow a woman to have relations with other men to produce children, as we see in the story of Ambika and Ambalika in the Mahabharata. In an economic downturn, it is said that the Brahmins can behave like the Kshatriyas, the Kshatriyas can behave like the Vaishyas. The Dharma-shastras give various examples on how this can be done, with the caveat that when the situation improves one must revert to one's traditional occupation. But does that ever happen?

For a long time, Indians didn't cross the sea, or kala paani, as they believed it resulted in the corruption/loss of one's caste. However, famine and an economic downturn in the nineteenth and early twentieth centuries forced Indians to seek employment outside. Therefore, the idea of kala paani was revoked. Today, people have no issue crossing the seas, because the world has changed enormously. Crisis has forced us to change our minds. An economic crisis forced India to liberalize its economy. The crisis passed, but it would not be advisable to pull back 'emergency reforms'; they have now become the norm. Economic crises force Indians to give up traditional vocations and migrate to cities and to foreign lands to do whatever they can to earn an income. The old jati system exists only in bigoted minds.

Bhishma, in his discourse on political economy, shows the need to change rules during a calamity, provided the fundamental principle of protecting and providing for the weak remains.

Most of us are staying at home during the pandemic, doing chores we perhaps would not do in normal circumstances. Men are, perhaps for the first time, doing the dishes, sweeping and mopping the floor. But are we providing for our maids and support staff who are also isolated at home or have been forced to migrate back to the village? Will we revert to old habits when the crisis passes? Drona, for one, was forced to become a warrior in hard times but he did not revert to being a priest when he acquired wealth.

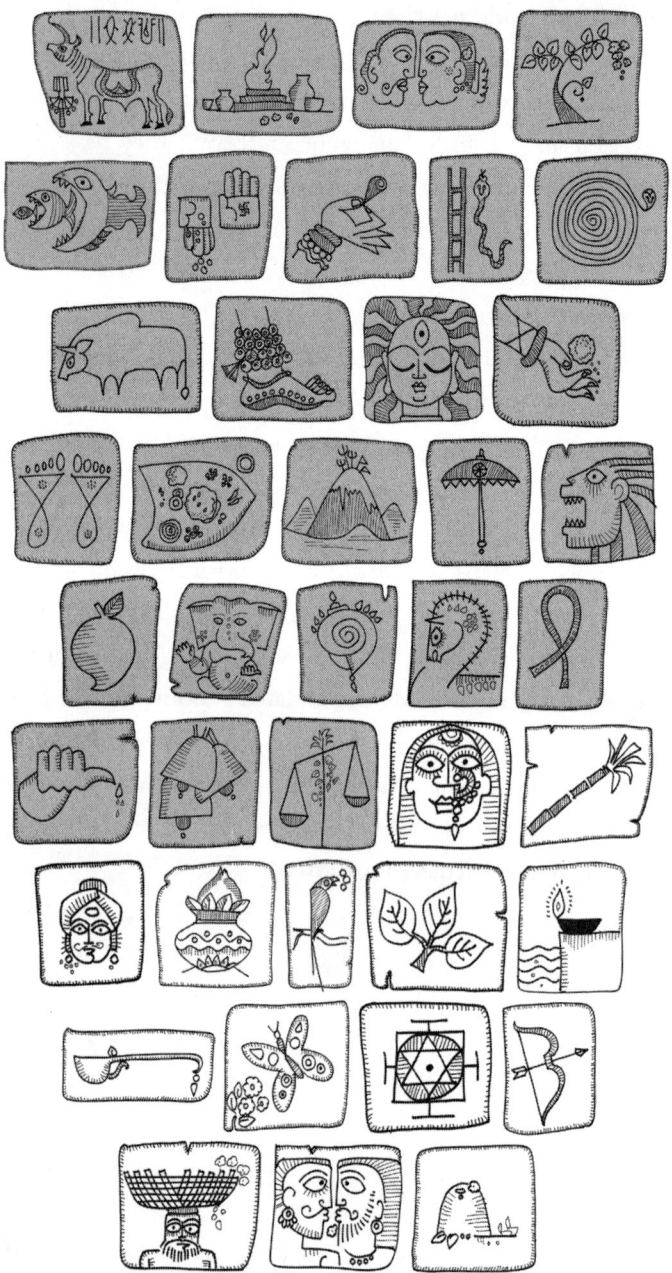

26

Artha
Can Sex-work Be Seen as Commerce?

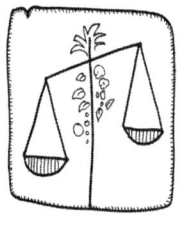

Shift the vowels slightly and the Sanskrit word for trader (vaishya) becomes the Sanskrit word for prostitute (veshya). One sold goods and the other sold pleasure. Both sought the highest bidder. Neither was loyal. Naturally, feudal authorities despised them both, and turned the word 'bazaru', or commercial, into an insult.

In all societies, there are two main sources of wealth: land and the market. Feudalism depends on land and trade depends on the market. Landowning communities (Kshatriyas) and trading communities (Vaishyas) have always competed for control of society. It accounts for the division between Old World Europe and New World America. Typically, feudal societies are hierarchical and value loyalty and patronage whereas trading societies are relatively egalitarian, giving greater value to the customer's wallet than to his status.

In India, we have sought to reject 'Old World Feudalism' but we have not yet embraced 'New World Free Trade'. We still value loyalty over merit. We are suspicious of professionals, because they sell their skills for a price, and we are fiercely independent, like prostitutes of yore. The traditional service-providers (Shudras) were expected to serve without expectation, accept patronage, but never demand payment, resulting in their semi-enslavement. Only priests (Brahmins) could demand a service-fee (dakshina), and a monk (bhikku) could demand alms (bhiskha). The rest were expected to live on the charity (daan) of the feudal master.

Further, the priests and monks of India consolidated their exalted status by establishing the doctrine of pollution and purity. This ensured their position at the top of the social pyramid, even above the landowning communities, but pacified the latter by locating them above traders and service-providers. A landowner could earn legitimacy and karmic dividends by paying priests and feeding monks. Travel, on the other hand, was deemed polluting, which is why many Indian traders stopped travelling and turned to moneylending. They outsourced the once-thriving sea-trade, at first to Arabs and later the Portuguese, for fear of loss of caste, a fear that prevented them from venturing out into the world right up to the twentieth century.

Service-providers whose vocation brought them into contact with blood, flesh, excrement and other bodily waste were deemed Untouchables, denied access to the village well and human dignity, because of the doctrine of pollution and purity. Lower than men were women who shed blood every month and who were recipients of semen, excreted by their husbands. And lower than all other women was the prostitute, who received the bodily fluids of many men, of all castes, for a fee.

But this was not always the case. As we have seen, there was a time when the prostitute was celebrated. The most beautiful woman in the city was not allowed to marry. She became the city-bride (nagar-vadhu). She was allowed to choose a lover, but did not have to restrict herself to one. That she chose the most handsome, the most powerful and, often, the richest, annoyed the less handsome, less powerful and less rich, who wrote poems about her heartlessness, while praising her beauty and skill. She was known for her singing, her dancing, her skill in conversation, her wit, her humour, and her beauty. We hear of these courtesans in ancient Hindu, Buddhist and Jain literature. Known as ganikas, they lived independent lives, unlike the chaste wives who lived in the shadow of their husbands, or nuns, who shunned all pleasure.

In time, these ganikas came to be attached to temples. They became wives of the enshrined deities; they were never widowed, and loved all men as containers of the divine seed. These were the devadasis. Their images inspired the carvings of beautiful women on temple walls. They challenged the old monastic orders. They were part of temple rituals.

But eventually, the priests and the monks stripped the devadasi of her independence and her agency. Gradually, she became answerable to the men in positions of power. These men declared how pure, or impure, she was. She was dirty because she had many lovers. She was dirtier because she went to the highest bidder. Eventually, she was just an exploited woman, with no freedom, her fee being claimed by a pimp or a madam.

If not attached to a temple, the woman who sold pleasure for a fee became part of a king or nawab's court, or a community of entertainers, the nats. In her world, skills and wealth were passed from mother to daughter. She could make money if she had the beauty, skill and guile. She was invited to weddings and coronations and festivals.

But status was another matter. In a feudal society, that looked down on trade and commerce, that created hierarchy based on purity of vocations and gender, she was clearly at the bottom. What little agency she had was taken away from her, first by colonial administrators and later by puritanical freedom fighters, who modelled themselves on the monks of yore.

Today, unlike the nineteenth century, no one fears loss of caste when one travels across the seas. Today, we are comfortable talking about markets, buying, selling, trade and profits. Today, we seek professionals. Yet, the feudal mindset persists.

We yearn for loyalty and are afraid of the commercial: those who sell their skills and expertise to the highest bidder. We cannot bear the thought of pleasure being a commodity that can be bought and sold. We prefer women who submit to the decisions of men, not women who make their own decisions. We prefer the loyal press and are terrified of an independent one who, like the independent ganika of yore, believes that their dharma is to treat all customers equally, no matter how much they are paid, and be loyal to none. That is why the press with a mind of its own becomes 'presstitute' and a lady politician with a mind of her own, who refuses to submit, becomes the veshya.

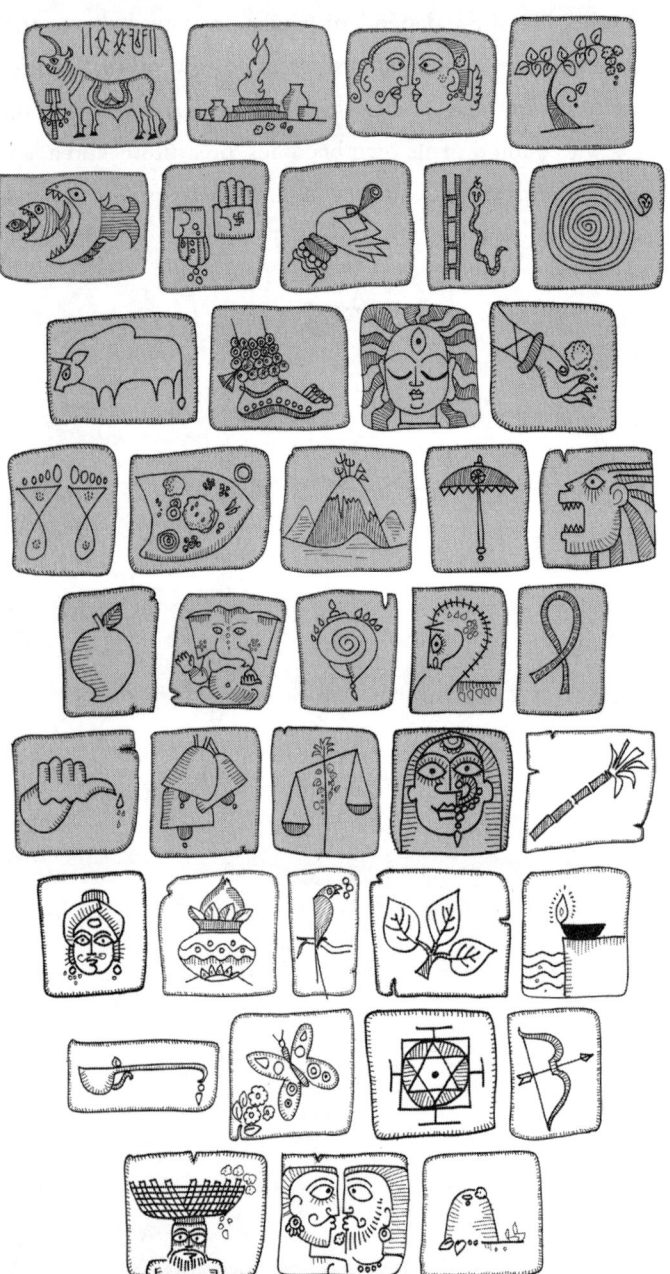

27

Kama
Desire and the Goddess

 In Buddhist belief, the greatest enemy of Buddha, who seeks to outgrow desire, is Mara, the demon of desire. In Hindu belief, Mara is Kama, the god of desire. Kama raises his sugar cane bow, shoots a flower arrow at Shiva, the hermit, lord of yoga, to ignite desire in him. But Shiva opens his third eye, releases a missile of fire and sets Kama aflame, reducing him to a heap of ash.

If Shiva does not marry, he will father no children and the demon Taraka will not be killed. Nothing will grow: the bee will not come to the flower, the bull will not go to the cow, the earth will be bereft of life. So, the Goddess comes to Shiva as Kamakshi. Her name is similar to Kama; she also bears the sugar cane bow and flower arrows of Kama. She dances on top of Shiva, she sits on him, appeals to him to open his eyes and accept her as his wife, not for his sake but for the sake of those who are terrorized by Taraka. Shiva finally opens his eyes; he becomes Shankara, the benevolent one, who marries Kamakshi, and they have a son called Kartikeya who kills Taraka.

In later Buddhist literature, Buddha becomes Bodhisattva, sprouting more arms, and embraces the goddess Tara who flavours his serene wisdom with more compassion.

The seed of any enterprise, any yagna, is desire or kama. Unless the yajaman has a desire, the yagna will never start. There will be no exchange, no marketplace. For wealth creation and wealth movement, there has to be bhoga, not yoga. In the modern world, marketing exists to destroy yoga and invoke bhoga. The yogi who seeks to withdraw from the world is the greatest threat to the marketplace. He has to be seduced. That is why Indra sends apasaras to seduce them. The hermit is engaged in solitary activity that distances himself from society. As householder, he becomes part of society, of exchange, of giving and taking.

In the Ramayana, when Dashrath wants to perform a yagna that will get him sons, he is advised to call the sage Rishyashringa. The sage has been raised all his life without knowledge of women. He has no hunger and nothing will compel him to leave his hermitage. So Dashrath sends Shanta, daughter of Lompada, to enchant him and bring him to Ayodhya. Shanta succeeds, Rishyashringa comes to Ayodhya, performs the yagna and Dashrath gets four sons. It is Dashrath's desire that leads to the seduction of Rishyashringa, the performance of the yagna, and the birth of Ram and his brothers. If Kama had not shot his arrow, if there was no desire for bhoga, there would be no Ram, no Ramayana.

It is not accidental that the word in Vedic literature for trader, vaishya, is very similar to the word for prostitute, veshya. Both were associated with the bazaar, the market: where Lakshmi is created and exchanged. That is why during festivals of the Goddess, clay is collected from the house of the veshya to make the image, and money from the house of a vaishya to prepare the pandal. They give shape to the centre of the celebration.

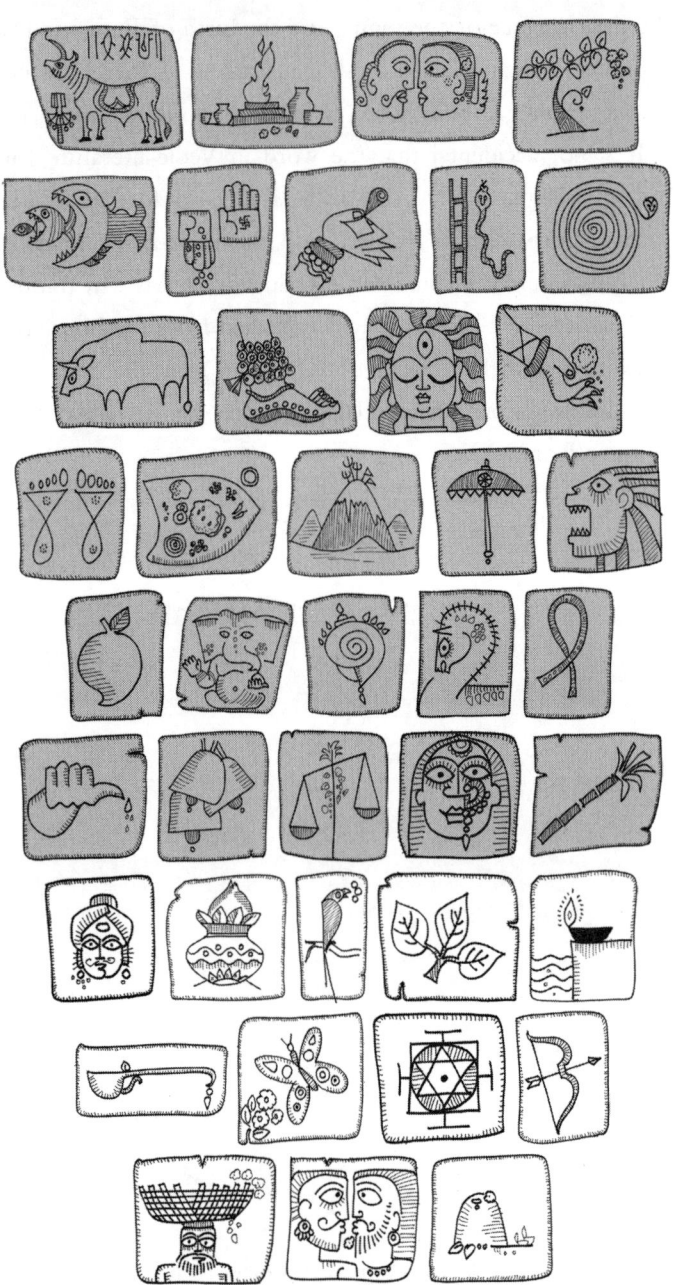

28

Moksha
Motivation of Kama and Yama

Shiva is called the destroyer because he destroys our desire—Kama—and he destroys death itself—Yama. Kama is associated with life and Yama with death. Shiva destroys both the desire for life and the fear of death and thus he is the god of liberation or moksha. Imagine a world where we don't have to do anything, and we don't want anything, where there are no aspirations or obligations. Then we create Kailash, the abode of Shiva, a world without wants or needs.

When we live like Shiva without any wants and needs, we have no desire for wealth or power or success or staff. That is why the ascetics of India have no home, no property, no relationships. They are a burden to no one, and they have no burdens. They have no debt. No one owes them anything. They are absolutely free.

Kama puts us in debt as he fills us with lust, desire, yearnings and longings. He makes us want to be rich, to have a bigger house, a bigger car, better clothes, to travel abroad, spend more money, have lavish weddings. When people become successful, they start outsourcing the work to other people because they can afford to do so and when they are very successful, they have a large staff.

In India, the first level of success means we have no staff; level two has part-time staff; level three has one full-time staff; and level four has multiple full-time staff. These are aspirations, wants. We don't necessarily need them, but we want them. It is Kamadeva who wants us to have ambition, to think big, to start businesses, to move from level one to level four. These are things we may want to accomplish but do not have to. Kama is an archer and his arrows that strike us fill us with sweet sorrow.

By contrast, Yama is about the things we do have to do. Yama embodies obligations. He is the keeper of debts. He forces us to be reborn till all debts are repaid. 'Hrinn' or debt is a very important concept in Hinduism. It is said that we are all bound by debt and the whole purpose of moksha or freedom is to be free of our debts. We owe our lives to our parents, our ancestors, our society and to nature at large and must repay all these debts before we can be truly free. Yama yokes everyone with his noose and does not let go. He is the grim accountant of karma.

Thus, we have these two forces in our lives. There is Kamadeva, who motivates us with desires and aspirations; and there is Yama, who propels us to uphold our obligations and responsibilities. If we ask ourselves why we work, we realize it is not always because of aspiration. It is often because of obligation. We work not because we want to work but because we have to work. When we are struck by Kamadeva's arrows, we have an inner drive. When we are bound by Yama's noose, there is no drive. Work is only a burden to bear.

It is often assumed that Kama motivates the privileged and Yama propels the unprivileged. But that is not true. Many rich people work as they are obliged by family expectations and many poor people do what they do because they like it, and not necessarily because it makes them money.

In the rainy season, across north India, young men are encouraged to carry water from the Ganga to their village temple in pots that must never be placed on the ground. This is the kavad. It is a metaphor for the obligations of life that they must carry as responsible householders. They may not be struck by Kama's arrows, but they are obliged by Yama's noose.

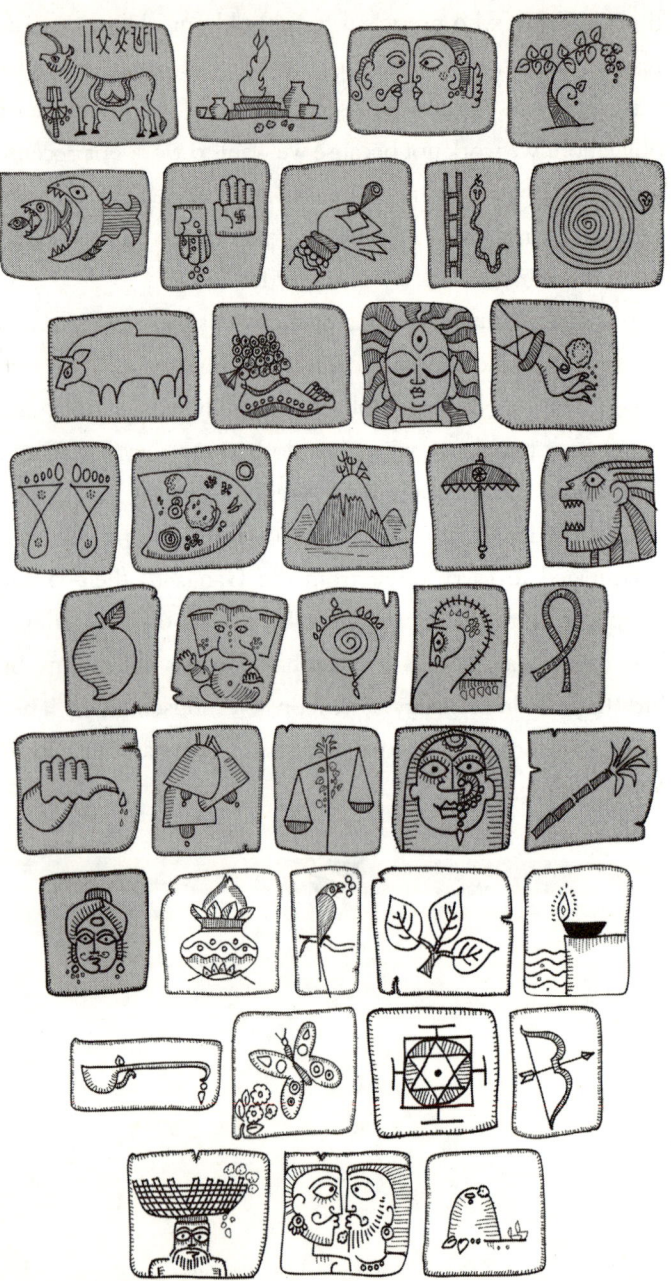

29

Dharma
Reimagining Caste

Courts today decide who is male, who is female, who is rich, who is poor, who is juvenile, who is mature, which sexual behaviour is appropriate and which is not, what is rape and what is consent. Not surprising for a country whose founding fathers (Gandhi, Nehru, Patel, Rajagopalachari, Prasad, Ambedkar) were all lawyers. This legal code was supposed to create a world that is more secure. I am told that before the legal system existed there was chaos and anarchy and oppression.

The Vedic hymn 'Purusha Shukta' describes every society as an organism whose head is made of Brahmins (intellectuals) who guide society, whose arms are made of Kshatriyas (warriors) who protect society, whose torso is made of Vaishyas (traders) who feed society, and whose legs are made of Shudras (service-provider) who serve society. Many social reformers believe this four-fold system is the root of evil in Indian society because it gives too much value to the Brahmins and is totally undemocratic.

But modern India has returned to this four-fold model because of, or despite, democracy. The lawyers, judges and thinkers make up the head (neo-Brahmins, like the priests of yore, who decide what is right); the politicians make up the arms (neo-Kshatriyas, like the kings of yore, who use force to get their way); the industrialists, corporates and entrepreneurs make up the torso (neo-Vaishyas, like the merchants of yore, who have money power); and then come the neo-Shudras, the activists who fight for human rights, citizen rights, environmental protection, rights of women, children, the disabled, queer, and elderly, and who challenge the higher varnas that have access to authority, power and money.

The neo-Brahmins are supposed to safeguard citizen rights, the neo-Shudras fight for it, and the neo-Kshatriyas and the neo-Vaishyas deny it as they go about cornering the nation's resources. In the Puranas, we hear stories of Brahmins rising up against greedy kings such as Vena. But do we see that in modern society? Criticizing neo-Brahmins is seen as 'contempt'.

Activists may not like being called a neo-Shudra (since it is lowest in the caste hierarchy), and judges may not like being called a neo-Brahmin (as it is politically incorrect). But the legal system has created a new four-fold system, whether we admit it or not.

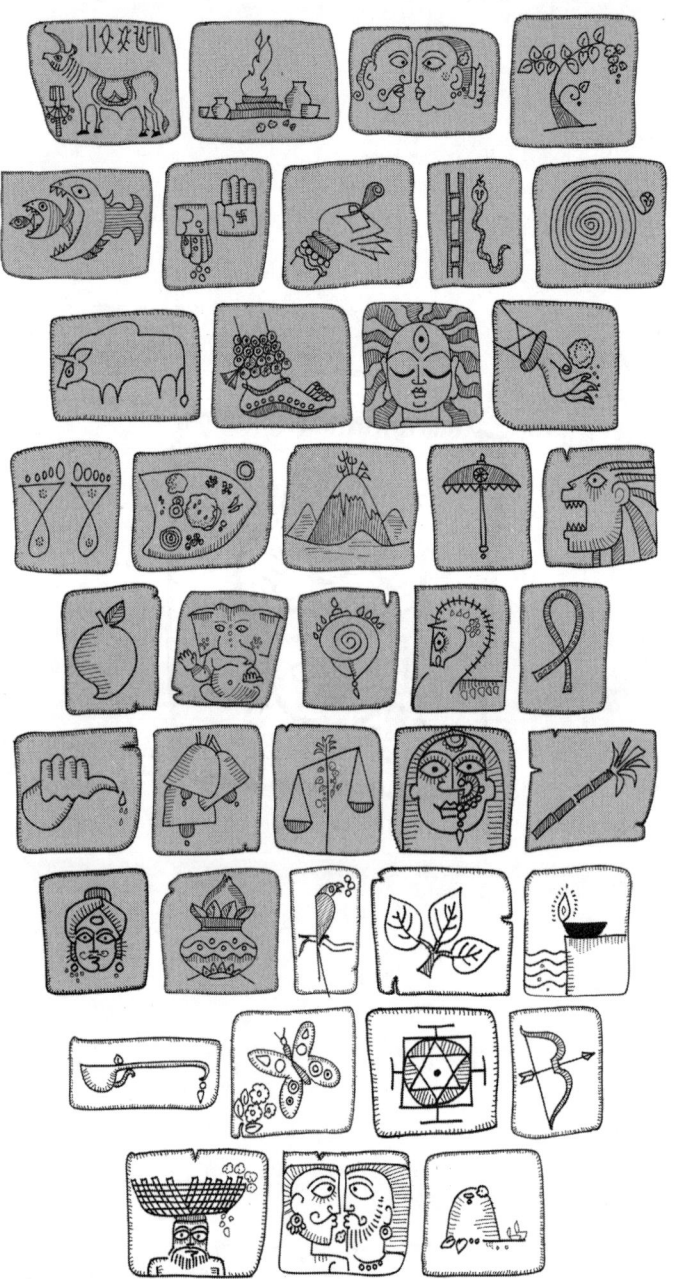

30

Artha
Demon Father

Lakshmi, goddess of wealth, has three fathers. There is Varuna, god of the sea, who gives the world salt, fish and all the water it needs. This is why Lakshmi is called Sagara-putri. Then there is Puloman, the asura-king, who rules from the subterranean realm of Patala, where the primary form of all wealth is located. This is why Lakshmi is called Paulomi and Patala-nivasini, or resident of Patala. Finally, there is Bhrigu, the sage who can see the future and hence bring fortune. This is why Lakshmi is called Bhargavi.

Varuna gives Lakshmi away freely without resentment; and so is blessed with abundance. Puloman resists giving Lakshmi away and keeps fighting with the devas, who want to make Lakshmi their queen, Sachi. Bhrigu rarely shares his secret and very reluctantly parts with his daughter. That is why for most humans Varuna is a generous god, worthy of worship, while Puloman is a demon and Bhrigu the guru of demons.

Wealth was visualized as a daughter that we create. She sits in our wallet. But she brings value only when she is given away. This is kanya-daan, giving away of the bride. To not part with wealth, to hoard, was considered the gravest of crimes. Yakshas, who hoard wealth, are therefore seen as demons, who are often attacked and tortured by their half-brothers, rakshasas, just as the devas are perennially at war with the asuras.

Through these stories value was placed on wealth distribution, allowing wealth to flow so that it brought in more value. It also revealed the mindset that was considered beneficial to society at large, and ultimately, to the individual involved in wealth generation.

Jamshed owns six bakeries across the city. Each bakery has a turnover of over two lakh rupees a day. But Jamshed does not care so much about the turnover. 'The more bakeries I build, the more boys and girls get jobs, the more people get to taste my bread and my cake. There is so much happiness in that,' he says.

Firoz is also in the baking business. He has two bakeries but he does not want to build more. He says, 'It is so much headache. The vendors do not give enough credit and the employees threaten to form unions. And the taxes are so high. Customers prefer Jamshed's breads to mine. He is too stiff a competition. I barely make profit.'

Shamsher also has a bakery that makes the most exquisite

scones in the city. There is always a crowd in front of his store. He does not share this recipe and makes the batter for the scones himself. He cannot expand the business, as he might have to share his trade secret. He is happy being exclusive and highly profitable.

Jamshed is like Varuna, who uses his money to take care of his employees and lavish his customers, who return the favour. Firoz is like Puloman: so careful about his money that both employees and customers feel the pinch. Shamsher is like Bhrigu whose customer-friendly ways ensure his success.

While all three generate wealth, Jamshed's wealth is shared amongst many people and it gives livelihood to many, reducing unemployment and helping society at large. The wealth of Firoz and Shamsher helps only them. They become rich. But when one is rich in a world where there is poverty and unemployment, one lives perpetually in fear, facing the resentment of the rest. This is unhealthy in the long run. We become 'demons' for other members of society.

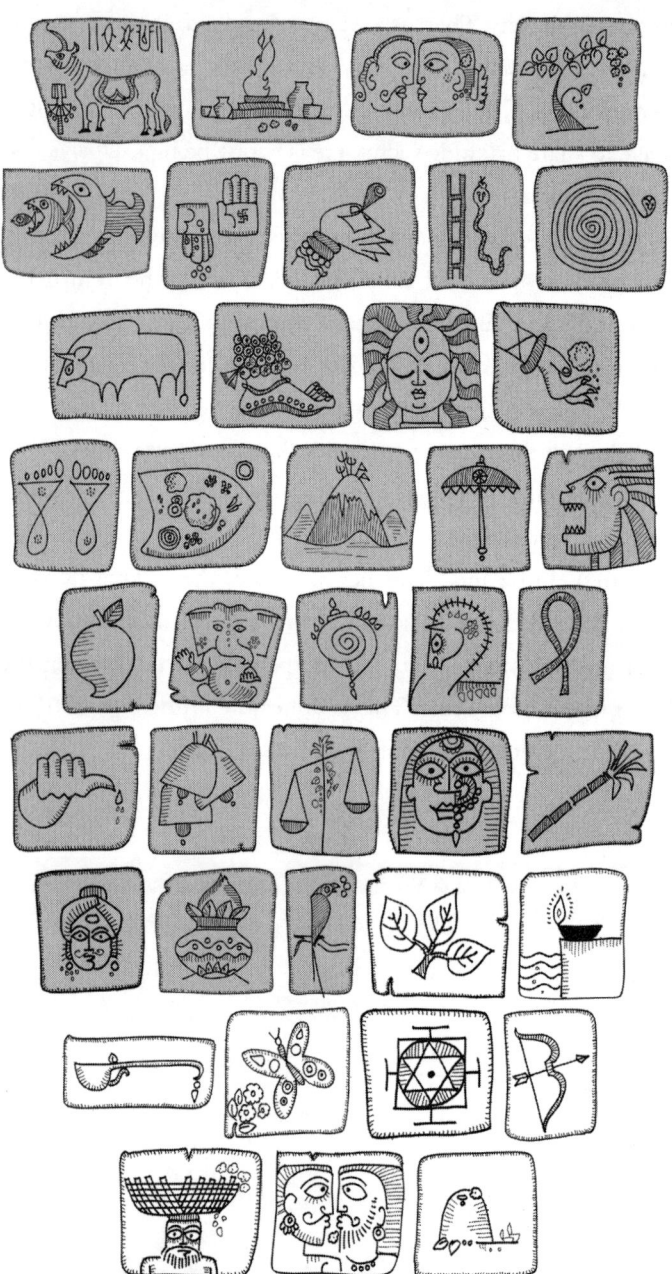

31

Kama
Power of Art

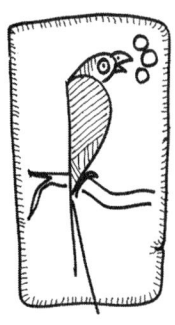 I remember the time my friend took me to the Kapaleeshwarar Temple in Chennai. It took the two of us almost an hour to reach the sanctum sanctorum. No, not because it was crowded, but because we were enjoying the vast range of Shaiva iconography that adorned the temple, from the gate through the corridors and right up to the innermost structure in which was located the enshrined deity. Meanwhile, dozens of devotees were rushing into the temple to get darshan and rushing out to do their daily chores. No one seemed interested in, or even aware of, the sophisticated art that embellished the temple walls. This art developed in India over 2,000 years, was codified in the Agamas, and was meant to communicate the Vedic view of life.

Somehow art appreciation is not seen as a religious or spiritual activity. The 'common man' is conditioned to be 'common' by rejecting all things deemed even slightly intellectual. But art appreciation is not an intellectual activity; it is a visceral activity. By looking at iconography we let the art evoke aesthetic sensations (rasa) and emotional outpourings (bhava) in our body. This is a valid means of non-cognitive transmission of the divine idea directly into our beings. Like champagne and caviar, or even single malt whisky, art appreciation is an acquired taste, a sign of high culture. Refinement is why art was so important in Hinduism. And it was made available to all.

I have seen many people bristling with rage at the idea that Muslim invaders broke Hindu temples and the British stole icons from India and took them to England, or that smugglers are stealing temple idols today and selling them in the antique black market. But I have seen very few who bristle at the thought that both they and their children are clueless about art appreciation of Indic iconography. Yes, they may be able to distinguish Durga from Lakshmi thanks to calendar art, but can they distinguish Chamunda from Charchika, or Yoga-Narasimha from Lakshmi-Narasimha?

At an Indian consulate in a foreign country a few years ago, I saw a Chola-era Shiva Pinaka-dhari (bow-holding Shiva) bronze statue being identified as Vishnu. 'Can't you see the third eye?' I asked the local official. The official did not know how to react. He was clearly clueless. 'Sir, please don't tell anyone or we will all get into trouble,' was the only thing he said. And so, Shiva still remains Vishnu, no thanks to a culture department full of officials more interested in bureaucracy than art appreciation.

We can blame the government and the education system, but how many parents actually take their children to museums, or temples, and play the game of 'let us identify this god'. How many Jain parents can actually take their children to a Jain mandir and together decipher the symbols of the various Tirthankaras, and identify the various yakshas and yakshis? How many of us know the difference between Gandharan Buddha and Mathura Buddha? Do we even care to find out where the oldest stone image of Ram or Krishna is? And no, it was not 5,000 years ago, and certainly not on the banks of the now-dry River Saraswati.

And then when European or American scholars write about these icons and call themselves experts, and foreign universities and museums publish their works in beautifully produced books, the bristling rage and outrage of patriotic Indians unleashes itself once again. In other words, our icons have been reduced to 'property'. Possessing them is more important than appreciating them. This is tragic.

As long as we do not appreciate our art, we will never notice it missing from temples. What gets lost is not a sacred object but a source of wisdom and beauty, an idea carved in stone, a moment of history frozen in time. Yes, we want to bring home the plundered treasures. But once home, can we spend some time looking at them a bit more curiously?

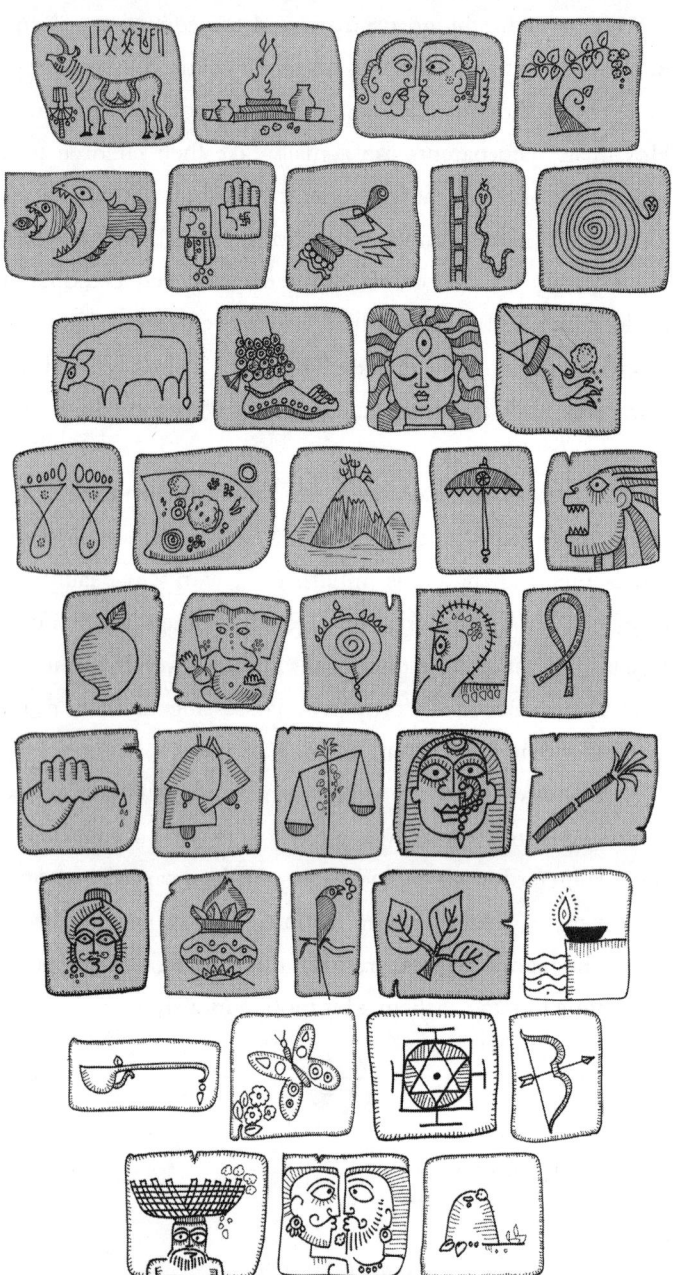

32

Moksha
Three Heavens of Hinduism

In traditional belief, there is only one Heaven.
This concept comes from monotheistic
religions—Christianity, Islam and Judaism—
all of which speak of one Heaven, the place where souls go
after death, if one has been true to the way of God. However,
in Hinduism, there is a reference to three heavens. There is
Swarga, the heaven of Indra; there is Vaikuntha, the heaven
of Vishnu; and there is Kailash, the heaven of Shiva. These
represent three very different concepts. None of these places
is accessible by following any law of God, because the idea
of commandments and alignment to the law of God are
Abrahamic concepts, not Hindu ones.

In the Vedas, there is no mention of Vaikuntha or Kailash;
these concepts come from a much later time: from the Puranic
traditions. In the Vedas, the performance of duties, especially

successfully carrying out of sacrifices and rituals such as yagna, enabled one's access to Swarga. In later traditions, references appear for the first time in the Mahabharata to the belief that one's time in Swarga is temporary and not permanent. There is a higher heaven beyond Swarga, which is referred to as Vaikuntha, the heaven of Vishnu. Similar ideas appear in the Puranas, wherein those who worship Shiva prefer Kailash to Vishnu's Vaikuntha.

If one observes the descriptions of Swarga, Vaikuntha and Kailash, one realizes they refer to very different psychological states. Indra's heaven is described as a place that has the wish-fulfilling tree, Kalpataru, the wish-fulfilling cow, Kamdhenu, the wish-fulfilling jewel, Chintamani, and a cornucopia of grain and gold known as the Akshaya Patra. In other words, Swarga is a place where all hunger is indulged, all our desires are fulfilled.

In contrast, Kailash, the heaven of Shiva, is a mountain of stone covered with snow, where nothing grows. There is no food here. Therefore, the only creatures who can survive in Kailash are those who are never hungry. Kailash is thus the abode of ascetics—those who have outgrown hunger. Since there is no hunger, Ganesha's mouse is not afraid of Shiva's snake, which, in turn, is not afraid of Kartikeya's peacock; Shakti's tiger is not interested in eating Shiva's bull, Nandi; and Nandi is not worried about the absence of grass on Mount Kailash.

Vaikuntha, on the other hand, lies on the ocean of milk, where Vishnu seems to live in luxury, reclining upon the coils of his serpent, with his spouse, Shree-devi, at his feet. While it looks like Swarga from outward appearances, Vishnu too, like Shiva, is not hungry—but he is paying attention to other people's hunger. This is why he does not stay in Vaikuntha forever, but descends from time to time, in various avatars (Ram and Krishna) to solve the problems on earth. He is, thus, interested in other people's hunger.

We realize the three Swargas in Hindu mythology are designed very differently from the single Heaven of Abrahamic mythology. Here, it is about the indulgence of hunger in Swarga, outgrowing hunger in Kailash and taking care of other people's hunger in Vaikuntha. Unfortunately, we sometimes confuse these concepts and are unable to appreciate that different cultures approach the idea of Heaven differently.

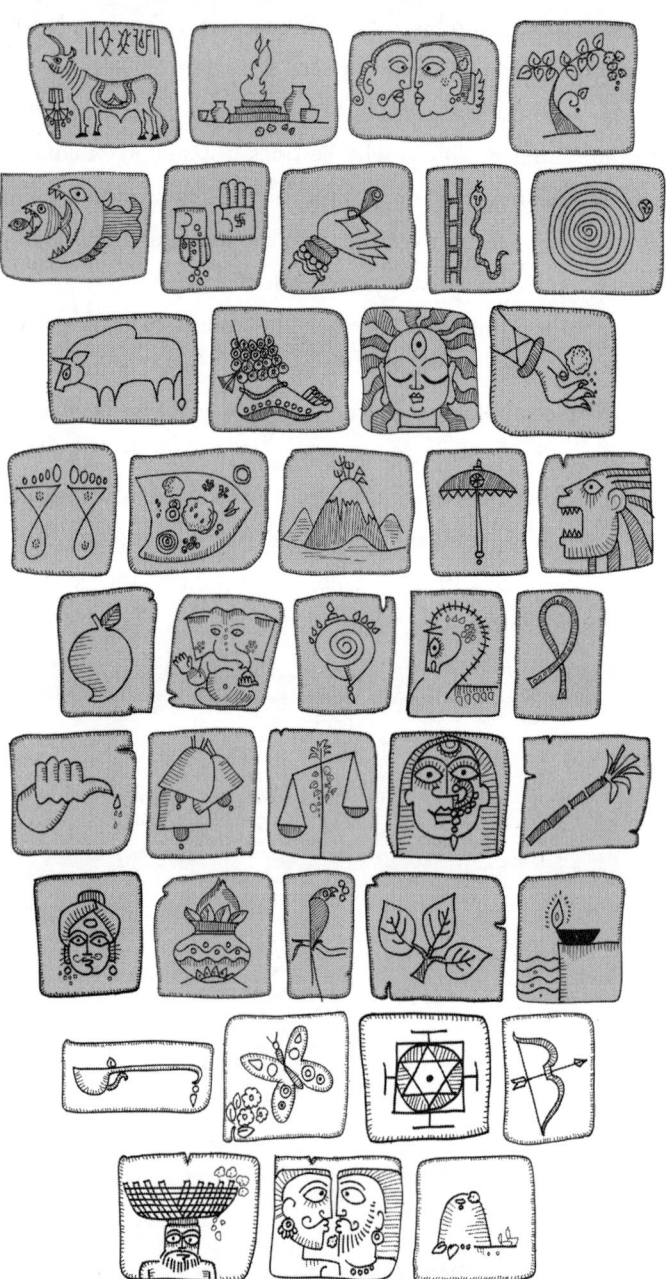

33

Dharma
Grow Up and Move On

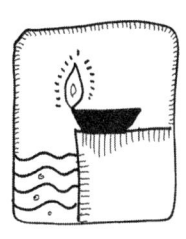 In Vedic times, life was divided into four stages: the first quarter was Brahmacharya-ashrama, the stage when one is a student; the second was Grihastha-ashrama, the stage when one is a householder; the third was Vanaprastha-ashrama, the stage when one retires from active household duty; the fourth was Sanyasa-ashrama, the stage when one detached oneself totally from the world.

Although it may not seem so on the surface, the ashrama-system is very much reflected in today's corporate world. When one takes up a job, one spends a lot of time learning the new job: this is Brahmacharya. Then a point comes when the learning stops and one becomes increasingly productive with higher and higher levels of efficiency and effectiveness: this is Grihastha. After that comes a time when one outgrows a job. One desires to move on. This is the stage when one must step into Vanaprastha, the twilight zone, when one empowers and enables the next generation to step in. Having created the talent pool that can take one's place, one achieves Sanayasa, the freedom to move on, out of the current job paradigm and into a new challenging paradigm. And the cycle starts all over again.

Conventionally, Vanaprastha is seen as retirement. But it can also be seen as the stage when one passes on one's skill and knowledge to the next generation, so that they can flourish while one moves on. The ashrama-system need not be applied only to one's professional life—it can be applied to each role one takes up. Thus, one has the four stages as an executive, then the four stages as a manager, then four stages as a director. If we want to grow, we must constantly keep retiring.

The perfect organization is said to be one that respects the march of the four stages. Where things move predictably—people move on and move in at the appropriate pace. This is celebrated in the Ramayana where, as soon as Ram completes his education, he is given a wife and, as soon as he marries, his father Dashrath declares his intention to retire, move out of the palace, and let Ram ascend the throne.

The ashrama-dharma in the Ramayana is a theoretical construct. It assumes that people are willing to move on to the next stage and they know when to move on. Life is not so simple. There are executives who do not want to be managers. And there are managers who will not let executives grow to be managers. And there are directors who realize they are quite ill-equipped to direct. This disruption in the orderly course is the theme of the Mahabharata.

The epic tells the story of King Shantanu who has a grown-up son called Devavrata, who is ready to marry and become king. But then Shantanu falls in love with a beautiful young fisherwoman called Satyavati. He wants to marry her but there is a condition: only her children should be declared his heirs. To Shantanu's great relief, Devavrata voluntarily gives up his claim to the throne. 'But what if your children fight my daughter's children?' asks Satyavati's father.

In response, Devavrata takes a vow never to marry, never to touch a woman and never to father or adopt a child. For this vow, the gods declare Devavrata to be 'Bhishma'. Bhishma is celebrated as the obedient son: a son who wants his father's happiness. Nobody condemns the father. As one reads the epic, one realizes that Bhishma's act of obedience is one of the prime reasons for the great carnage on the battlefield of Kurukshetra. If the older generation had made way for the younger generation, as the scriptures advised, the Mahabharata would not have happened.

The Mahabharata also tells the story of King Yayati who was so desperate to stay young that he begged one of his sons to suffer old age in his stead so that he could cling on to youth. His eldest son, Yadu, refused this request. The youngest, Puru, agreed. For obeying his father, Puru was made Yayati's heir (the Kauravas and the Pandavas are his descendants). For disobeying, Yadu was cursed that neither he nor his descendants would ever be kings (which is why

Krishna, of the Yadu clan, is always kingmaker, never king).

As in the Ramayana, this story of Yayati in the Mahabharata clearly celebrates the obedience and submission of the younger generation to the older generation. But there is one crucial difference. In the Ramayana, the older generation is not behaving like a parasite—they are willingly making way for the next generation. In the Mahabharata, the older generation takes advantage of the obedience of the younger generation to indulge their appetite for power and pleasure.

Organizations need to constantly look out for Yayatis and Shantanus—people who refuse to move on, who refuse to let the juniors grow. Those who use hierarchy to dominate and control rather than simply to maintain order and stability.

Take the example of Jaisingh. He is a brilliant store manager. And he is comfortable in this position, so comfortable that very deliberately he keeps mocking and demotivating his juniors, telling them how they are not fit to get a promotion and doing nothing to help them grow. He fears that if they learn how to be store managers, he will become redundant and be kicked out by the management. What the organization does not realize is that Jaisingh is behaving exactly like his boss, the regional manager Vijaysingh, who is fearful that Jaisingh will make him redundant. Both Jaisingh and Vijaysingh are stuck in Grihastha. Neither wants to move into Vanaprastha. Because both fear Sanyasa.

Letting go, moving on, is perhaps the most important skill one needs to possess in the corporate world. Imagine the human pyramid created during the Krishna festival of dahihandi to help the one on top get to the pot of curds and butter tied high up. Unless those at the lowermost level rise up, the one on top will never get to the butter. Ask yourself—are you rising to help your boss reach the pot? Ask yourself—are you allowing those below you to rise? Unless you do, the pot will never be yours.

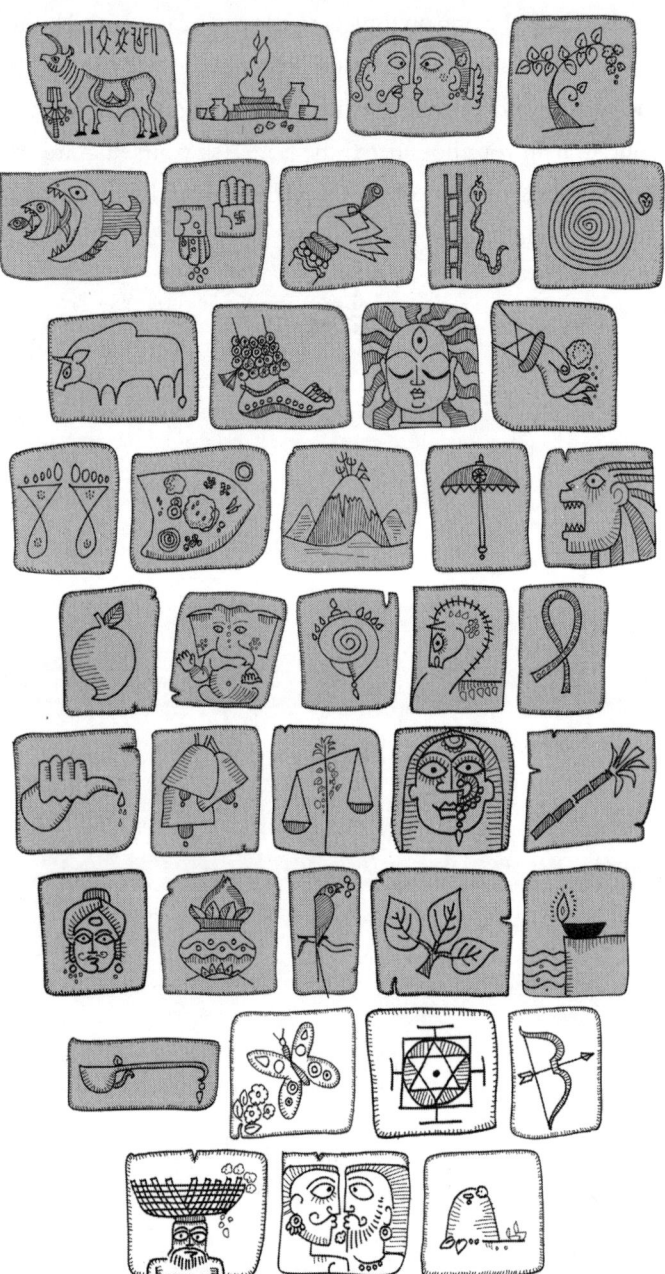

34

Artha

Brahmins—Kingmakers of South India and Southeast Asia

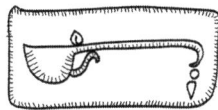 It is fashionable nowadays to use the word 'Brahmin' with contempt, inverting the contempt of many Indian elites for lower castes. It mirrors the contempt for all things 'white' seen in the intellectual West. One can say this is social justice at work, a pushback against centuries of Brahminical and white hegemony. But this outrage (real and imagined) must not blind us to the contribution of Brahmins, especially their role in creating the temple-states in south India and even across the sea in Southeast Asia.

To understand the role of religion in state formation, we must glance at the history of Ghana (eighth century) and Mali (thirteenth century) in west Africa and of the Swahili people (tenth century) in east Africa, where the arrival of Islam changed the fortunes of old city-states and trade routes.

For along with religion came philosophers and thinkers who understood economic and political systems, as well as art and architecture. Likewise, the migration of adventurous Brahmins, along with Buddhist and Jain monks, from north India to south India and thence to Southeast Asia, played a key role in the spread of the Indic civilization.

From around 300 CE to 1300 CE, from the Gupta period to the arrival of Islam in India, the elite from Afghanistan to Vietnam spoke Sanskrit and this shaped the kings as well as kingdoms in the region. This period saw the spread of Buddhism and post-Vedic 'Puranic' Hinduism to a vast part of the world, which is why when one visits Myanmar, Cambodia, Thailand, Laos or Indonesia, we feel a sense of civilizational continuity with India.

Since ancient times, people from north India had been travelling to Central Asia in the west and Southeast Asia in the east. But cultural contact was accelerated when religious ideas rose and began to spread. Amongst the first 'missionaries' were Buddhist monks, sent by Emperor Ashoka. Even before the Buddhists, from around 800 BCE, if not earlier, the men we refer to as Vedic rishis travelled to unknown lands over hills and forests and seas, spreading Vedic ideas beyond the Gangetic plains. Thus, we hear of Agastya rishi travelling to the south, having caused the Vindhya mountains to 'bend'. And we hear of Kaundinya rishi travelling to Cambodia and marrying a naga princess there.

Over time, from around 1,800 years ago, local chieftains started inviting Brahmins from the Gangetic plains to help set up kingdoms. These Brahmins were different from the Vedic Brahmins. They followed the Agama tradition based on the worship of Shiva and Vishnu in temples. They were knowledgeable in dharma-shastra (governance), artha-shastra (economics), niti-shastra (politics), kama-shastra (art), natya-shastra (theatre) and shilpa-shastra (architecture), and they were world-affirming.

They connected the clan gods (kula devatas) of the chieftains to Shiva, Vishnu and, most importantly, Durga, and brought them into the Hindu fold. Across India, even today, there are many kings known for venerating and tracing their power to a fierce goddess, often one who rides a lion or a tiger, such as Chamunda of Mysore, Bhavani of Kolhapur or the Thakuranis of Odisha, all of whom rose to popularity in the post-Gupta era.

These Brahmins helped a chieftain become a king by establishing a kingdom that privileged them and their clan. They were like Brihaspati to Indra and Shukra to Bali, priests in mythic texts. Historians call this process 'Kshatriyization' or 'Rajputization' where a king's ancestry was traced either to the sun (Surya-vamsa) and hence to Ram, the moon (Chandra-vamsa) or to fire (Agni-kula).

Land was given to Brahmins as donation (brahmadeya or agrahara), as indicated by the vast number of copper plates from this period. Brahmins established villages on these lands, inviting people of different communities to join them. These communities were organized in segments, based on vocation and hierarchy. The Brahmins, the kings and the aristocracy lived closest to the temple. At the margins lived the least powerful service-providers. In between were the markets.

Thus, we find across south India and Southeast Asia, from Kanchi in Tamil Nadu to Puri in Odisha and Angkor Wat in Cambodia, vast cities that grew around temples. To ensure the king did not feel threatened, the Brahmins made sure they were educated about the philosophy of 'detachment' and actively distanced themselves from profit and power. They focused on the deity in the temple and through him/her connected with the king. Internally, amongst Brahmins, the 'ritualist philosopher' gained higher status than the 'service-provider'. Eventually, the order of Brahmin-monks (matha, akhara) rose and became even more powerful than Brahmin-householders.

But this remarkable system had a negative side. At the periphery of these temple-states were communities of people involved in 'impure' vocations; they were ostracized and shunned to protect the core of mystical power that lay at the royal centre of the temple-state. Although many Brahmins such as Dyaneshwara and Eknath in Maharashtra, especially during the Bhakti movement, denounced this practice as being against the spirit of the Vedas, they failed to purge it. In time, this Brahminical obsession with 'purity' led to its global criticism and eclipsed its grand achievements in temple-states across South and Southeast Asia.

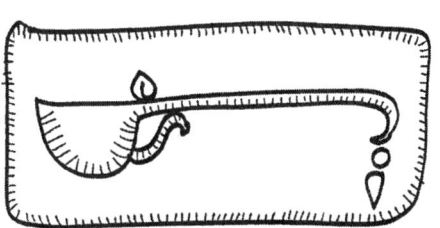

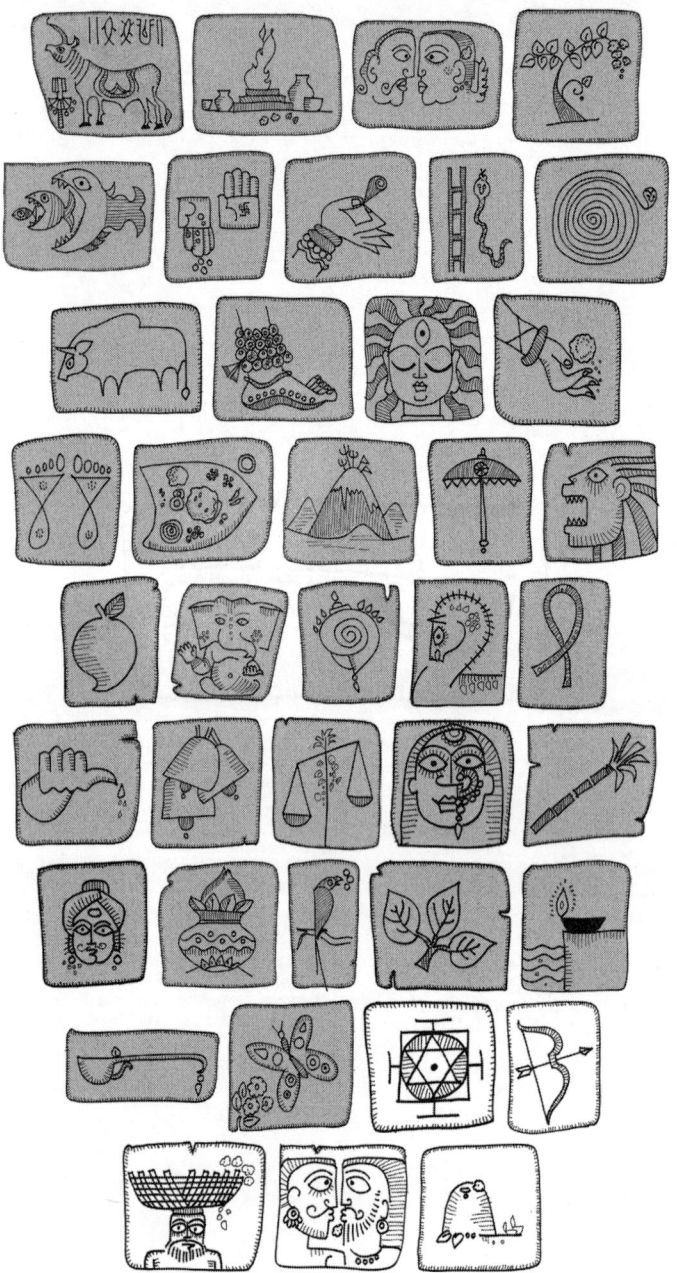

35

Kama
Four Types of Sex

Hindu texts often declare that the four goals of human life are dharma (ethics), artha (wealth), kama (pleasure), and moksha (liberation). However, as one goes through Hindu scriptures one finds different types of sexual activity that can easily be classified as dharma sex, artha sex, kama sex, and moksha sex.

In dharma sex, the purpose of sexual activity is only procreation. There is no love here, no desire and no attachment, just duty. The man approaches the woman during her ovulatory period with the sole intention of conceiving a child in her womb—only when she invites him, for only she knows when her body is most ready to conceive. When she approaches a suitable man, whether he is her husband or not, he is obliged to do the needful; if he does not, he is cursed.

We see this form of sex between rishis and their wives. Diti, for example, approaches Kashyapa at a time that is reserved for his evening prayers. Kashyapa is obliged to go to her but warns that the children born of the union will be asuras. Thus are Hiranyaksha and Hiranyakashipu born. Kashyapa cannot say no, as his wife has approached him during the ovulatory period making this dharma sex.

In another story, Kardama obliges Devahuti, his wife, and has sex with her only for the purpose of having a child. After she conceives, he retires to the forest. Eventually Devahuti gives birth to Kapila muni who is renowned for his Samkhya philosophy. Finally, there's Vyasa rishi, who goes to the widows of Vichitravirya during their ovulatory period upon the instructions of his mother, Satyavati, to ensure they conceive sons.

In kama sex, the purpose is pleasure and nothing else. Here, the focus is to indulge the senses and excite the mind and achieve orgasm. Homosexuality falls in this category, as it has no procreative purpose. This is also what the apsaras lure the rishis with. Kama, the god of desire, is feared as a great warrior who defeats the mightiest of sages. He has only faced defeat before Shiva, the supreme ascetic, no one else. So, it is ironic that Shiva is the fountainhead of the *Kamasutra*, the treatise on lovemaking. It was transmitted by Nandi, Shiva's bull—who witnessed the lovemaking of Shiva and Shakti, or overheard their conversation on the erotic arts—and was eventually put down in writing by sages such as Shvetaketu, Babhravya, Dattaka and, finally, Vatsyayana.

Kama sex is seen as a lethal force that can distract the ambitious from their goal. Thus, Vishnu takes the form of Mohini and with merely the promise of pleasurable intimacy tricks the asuras so that they are denied a share of Amrita, the nectar of immortality. Tilottama, an apsara, uses it to cause a fight between the asura brothers Sunda and Upasunda. And finally, there's Agnivarna, the last scion of the famous Raghu clan to which Ram belongs, who falls victim to the excesses of kama sex and dies a premature death, according to Kalidasa's *Raghuvamsa*.

In artha sex, sex is a transaction. It is used as a service offered in exchange for material favours. This was most commonly practiced by women known as ganikas or courtesans who provided all kinds of pleasure to men who were willing to pay for their services. But it was not restricted to ganikas. In the Mahabharata, Satyavati's father offers his daughter to Shantanu only on the condition that Shantanu make her children the heirs to his throne. There is also the story of Yayati offering his daughter Madhavi to any king in exchange for two hundred horses. Thus, sex becomes a commercial transaction.

In the *Kathasaritsagara* is the story of a handsome man who is invited to make a girl pregnant, as her husband has died and she needs a child; he is paid handsomely for it. In another folk story, a man who marries a widowed queen becomes the king. Thus, artha sex is not restricted to women alone.

Finally, there is moksha sex, wherein sex is seen as a way to break free from the unending cycle of birth and death.

This idea is prevalent in tantric texts where sex is not about pleasure or procreation or commercial transaction, rather it is about gaining magical powers known as siddhi that enable one to control nature. In the Bhagavata one hears of Lakshmi seated on the lap of Datta, son of Atri and Anasuya, who holds a bowl of liquor in his hand, and is busy in secret rites that escape the understanding of the sages who chance upon him. King Yadu learns that despite appearances Datta is cool and not burned by the fire of sexual desire, thus indicating his wisdom and liberation.

In the narratives of Matsyendranath and Gorakshnath one often hears reference to yoginis who live alone in the kadali vana or banana grove, who have access to occult powers, and who will offer these only to one who is capable of having sex with them. This idea is found in the stories of Padmasambhava, who took Buddhism to the Himalayan region, too. Tara reveals this knowledge to Bodhisattva; Shakti reveals it to Shiva; and Lakshmi reveals it to Datta, the ascetic form of Vishnu.

People argue if making love, or sex born of affection and love where the desire is simply to please the partner can be called kama sex or moksha sex. No one is sure even though it is clear that in this kind of lovemaking the ego takes a backseat.

Thus, we find sex being seen in different ways in ancient Hindu scriptures. For the sages, dharma sex was recommended so that they could procreate and have children thereby pleasing their ancestors without breaking the vow of celibacy. Kama sex and artha sex belonged to the householders. Moksha sex was reserved for the sages who followed the 'left-hand' path associated with Tantra.

36

Moksha
Peace, Peace, Peace

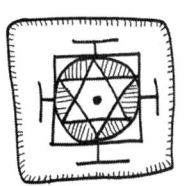

Every Hindu ritual ends with the three words 'Shanti, Shanti, Shanti-hi', a phrase conventionally translated as 'Let there be peace, peace, peace'. Why is the word repeated twice? And can there truly be peace in the world?

To assume that a world of peace can ever exist is considered naive in Hinduism. In order to survive, every creature needs food. To get food, animals have to turn into predators and kill. Violence plays a key role in supporting life. As long as there is need for food, there will be predation, hence violence, hence no peace.

Humans kill more than any other living creatures because we hoard more food than we need to survive, to insure ourselves against future scarcity. Every field, orchard, garden that provides us with food is established by destroying a preexisting ecosystem. Raw materials for industry can only be provided by destroying ecosystems. Human society is thus built on violence. Hinduism acknowledges this truism, which is why Hindu gods bear weapons in their hands. With such a pragmatic approach to violence, why do Hindu rituals repeat this chant for peace? And why is 'shanti' uttered three times?

In Shiva temples, the bilva sprig is offered to Shiva. The sprig has three leaves. Shiva's sacred mark comprises three horizontal lines. Shiva holds a trident which has three spikes. Shiva has three eyes—the left, the right and the all-powerful third eye. He is called Tripurantaka—destroyer of the three cities. Perhaps the secret of the chant for triple peace rests here.

Shiva is the archer who struck down three cities with a single arrow. The bow is the symbol of balance. To wield it one needs focus. To shoot three cities with a single arrow, one needs to be patient and aware of when the three cities are perfectly aligned. All these characteristics suggest that Shiva's archery is a metaphor for yoga. Yoga quietens the mind so that we are aware, patient, balanced and focused. In this state, we discover the three cities that we inhabit.

The three cities are our body, all things over which we claim ownership, and all things over which we do not claim ownership. In other words, 'me, mine and not-mine'. Ownership is a human delusion—humans believe they have legitimate rights over the earth and hence have the notion of property that we can possess, buy, sell and bequeath to the next generation. Property is a cultural concept, not a natural one. This is humanity's great delusion.

Yoga helps us realize that we own nothing in his world. We are born without possessions and we die without them. Realizing this we destroy the 'mine and not mine'. Yoga also helps us realize that 'me' is not the body. We have a false identity, aham or the ego, that depends on the body and will die, and a true identity called atma or the soul, that does not depend on the body and will never die. True wisdom makes itself accessible when we outgrow our dependence on 'me, mine and not-mine'.

So, the chant 'Shanti, Shanti, Shanti-hi' does not mean 'Let there be peace, peace, peace'. It means: 'Let me come to terms with the limitations of me, mine and not mine.' This is the ultimate goal of Hinduism: to outgrow aham and realize atma.

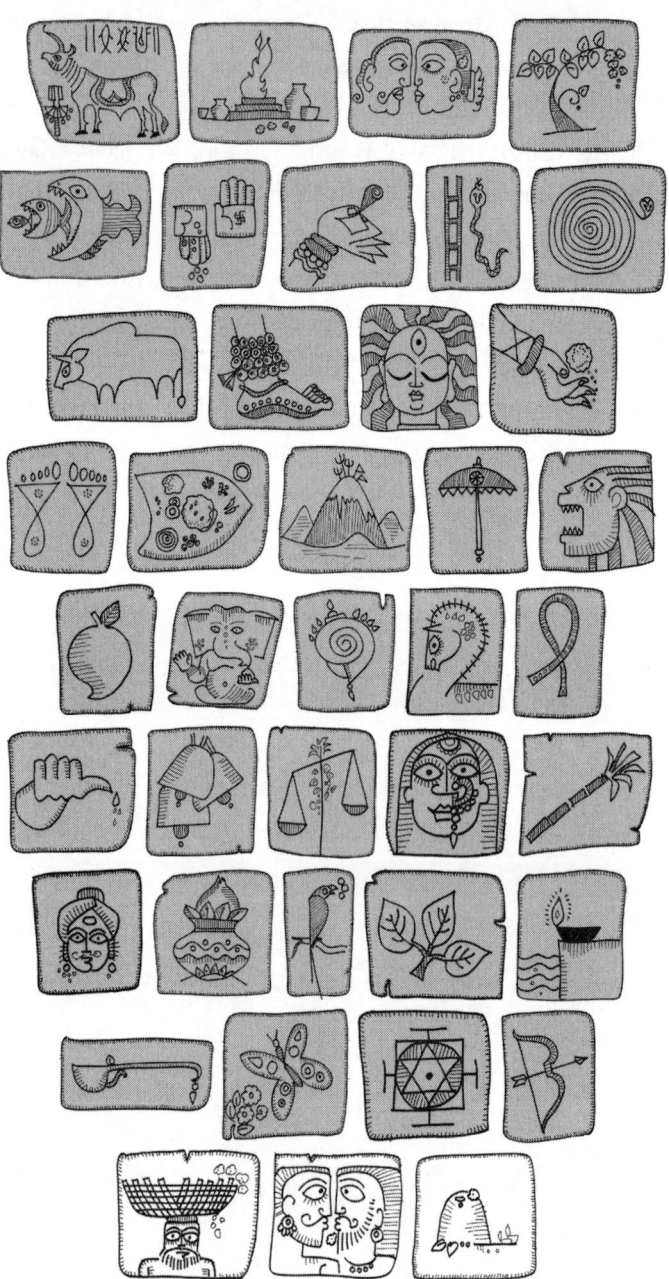

Dharma
Consequences of Justice

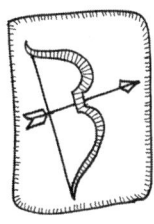The two ideas of 'justice' and 'forgiveness' may shape our understanding of conflicts, but Hinduism, which is based on karma, is more complex. Whenever we are deeply hurt, a question comes to our mind: ought we to seek justice through retribution, or should we let it go?

Justice and forgiveness are two concepts that really come to us from the Bible. In the Judeo-Christian-Islamic framework based on Abrahamic mythology, God is the Ultimate Judge. The Old Testament speaks of 'an eye for an eye', which is about justice and vengeance. The New Testament speaks about 'turning the other cheek' if slapped on one, which basically refers to forgiveness. These two ideas shape our global understanding of conflict and diplomacy.

People have tried to use the same framework to appreciate

the Hindu response to a crisis. Therefore, when there is a crisis, people need either justice or a compromise for peace to attain eventual happiness.

Hinduism is based on karma: every event that happens before us, or to us, is the result of the seeds we sowed in the past. Hence, we must take responsibility for events which happen in our lives. Taking responsibility, however, is the toughest thing in the world.

Let's understand karma by looking at the epics, the Ramayana and the Mahabharata. The Ramayana begins with the story of Valmiki watching two birds, one of whom is shot and killed. The surviving bird mourns the death of her beloved. Valmiki is so upset by this event that he curses the hunter. The bird cannot curse, it only knows how to grieve.

This event draws attention to the difference between animals and humans, nature and culture. In nature, there is no concept of justice or forgiveness, there is only suffering. Humans, however, can compensate for suffering by demanding justice or forgiveness. Or maybe there is something else, because the human mind is capable of imagining a world of karma where every event occurs because it's supposed to occur: there is no one to blame and, therefore, no one to forgive.

When Ram kills the monkey-king Vali and the demon-king Ravana, their wives are devastated. In many retellings, Vali's widow, Tara, and Ravana's widow, Mandodari, curse Ram that he too will face separation from his beloved spouse. This has been cited as the reason for Sita's banishment from Ayodhya. Ram pays the price for his military victory, however righteous his war may or may not have been. He does not complain about it.

Likewise, in the Mahabharata, everybody speaks of how Krishna establishes dharma by getting the Pandavas to defeat the Kauravas. However, we rarely speak about the collateral damage: the death of Draupadi's children, Arjuna's son Abhimanyu and Bhima's son Ghatotkach; how Gandhari curses Krishna and his entire clan is eventually wiped out. Krishna does not complain. Even a dharmic war has collateral damage, which the gods accept without getting upset. Consequences are a part of life.

This worldview is very different from the outlook that demands justice or forgiveness. In the world of Ram and Krishna, every action has a reaction. One learns that the negative events in our lives are the outcome of our past actions. If we respond to these events, we sow fresh seeds, which lead to positive or negative outcomes. The seed and the fruit follow each other in a timeless cycle unless we step back and witness life, like the sages and gods do. We often discuss how Ram and Krishna established dharma, but we rarely speak about both being cursed by the women hurt by the violence.

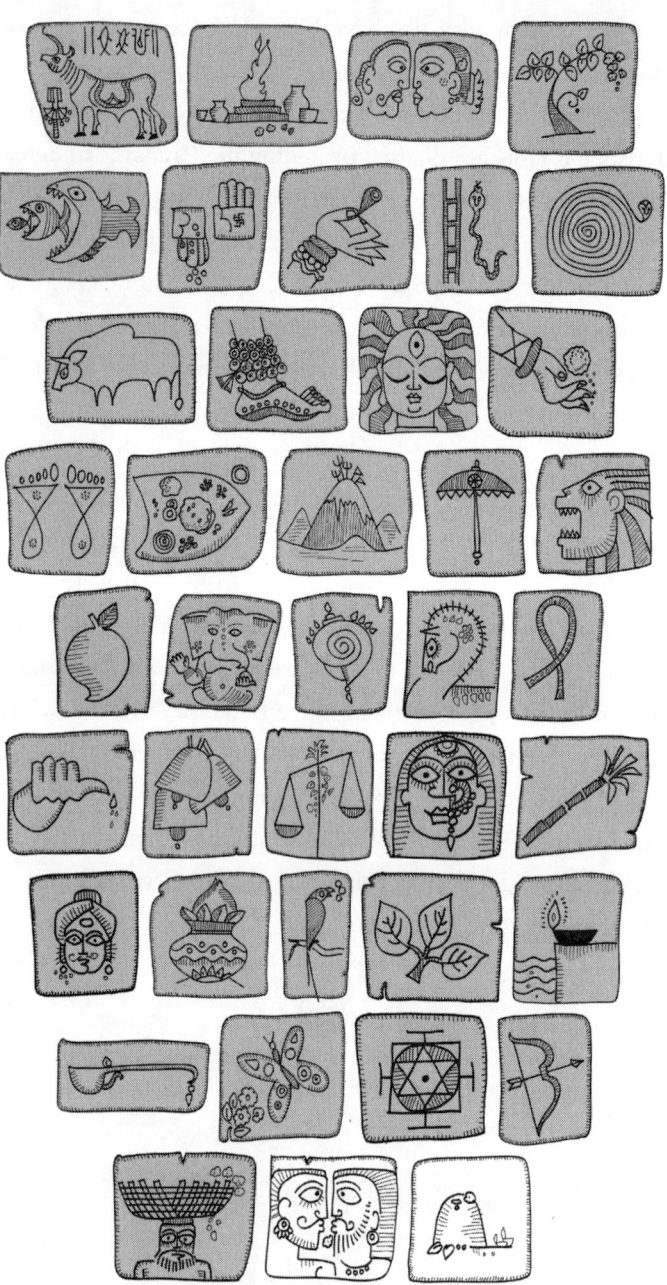

38

Artha
The Shudra Inside

The gesture of 'namaste' means to salute the divine within people. It is also a gesture of humility, submission and petition before power. Namaste between equals has the former meaning but the latter meaning is evoked through the namaste of a junior to a senior, of a servant to a master, of a student to a master, of a child to a parent. It is a simple gesture that expresses power dynamics in religious, spiritual as well as social contexts.

In Bhakti poetry, we often use the word 'malik' or 'nath' (both of which mean master) for god. Meera tells Krishna to keep her as his 'chakar' or servant. Those who do free service for gurus and temples, are happy to be 'dasa' and do 'seva'. Dasa-bhaav, or emotion of servitude, displayed by Hanuman towards Ram is seen as a form of passionate devotion that unites the jiva-atma of the devotee with the param-atma of the deity. Many argue this is a reminder of how feudal India was and how such approaches to the divine seem to normalize patriarchy. We don't mind serving the divine, or serving gurus and acharyas, but do we treat our servants and service providers with respect? If we did, would we see Shudra varna as the 'lowest' varna?

In the Vedas, the Brahmins who perform rituals are seen as the head of the Purusha, while the Shudras form the feet. In the Gita, a Shudra is described as one who serves the other three varnas. When we choose to serve, it can be seen as an exercise in humility. But when one is bound to serve, with no choice whatsoever, it is humiliating. It is rather patronizing when someone from the upper varna tells a Shudra that there is glory in serving.

In ancient India, Brahmins acquired power through education and access to the Vedas, Kshatriyas acquired power by controlling land, and Vaishyas acquired power by producing and trading products. Shudras, however, provided services. Skilled services were ranked higher than unskilled ones. In all these societies, skilled service-providers such as potters, metalsmiths, weavers, carpenters, barbers and washermen did have greater power than unskilled labourers. As the 'doctrine of purity' evolved, those engaged in 'unclean' professions such as butchers, tanners and sweepers were further sidelined from power, even dehumanized through the practice of untouchability, something that unfortunately continues in the misguided name of purity and holiness.

In temple towns, those who lived in the centre had the most power and purity; those who lived on the edge had the least. So deeply entrenched is this idea of caste purity that in some cities of Pakistan, an Islamist state, one hears about communities of sweepers and sewer cleaners who are perceived as dirty and inferior, and are not allowed to convert to Islam, as that would make them 'equal'.

In ancient India, 'dasi-putra' or son of a slave-woman was a term of derision. The term 'servant' or 'naukar' remains an insult in society. During the Bhakti period, many saints called themselves Shudra-muni and challenged caste hierarchy, insisting that in the eyes of God all are equal. But today, if anyone speaks for the service class, he or she is often branded as Marxist and Leftist and thus anti-national.

In pre-industrial societies there was no concept of social mobility; one's fate was very much decided at birth. But in industrial society, we are told that everyone should have equal opportunities and choices. Be that as it may, in the end, we all have to be 'useful' to society and provide goods or services. Which means we are either product-sellers and traders, the Vaishya, or service-providers, the Shudra. Words like Brahmin and Kshatriya are merely cosmetic and nostalgic.

Today, teaching is a service, as well as serving in the army, in the bureaucracy or a corporation; hospitality is a service, doctors are also serving, as are cooks and cleaners, accountants, drivers, and so on. Yet, we do not consider the service class as Shudras. Isn't a businessman who provides outsourcing services to international clients technically a Shudra? Isn't a soldier or politician serving the nation also a Shudra? Isn't a journalist who serves the public by speaking truth to power a Shudra? If everyone serves the nation, are we not all Shudras?

If we flinch at the thought, we have to ask ourselves why? For it reveals hierarchies we cling on to. Why do we classify some services as Shudra and others as non-Shudra? Even today we celebrate the rise of Karna from charioteer to archer as a sign of social mobility. But how many of us are comfortable describing Krishna the cowherd and Krishna the charioteer as a service-provider?

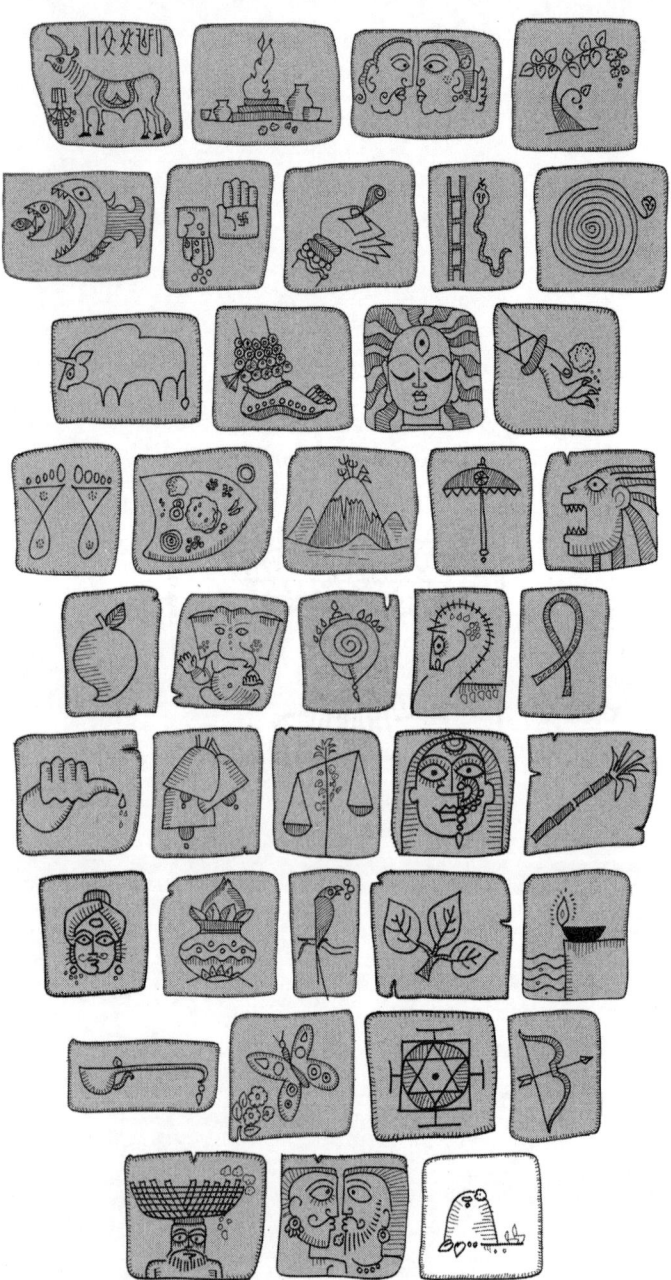

39

Kama
Queer Indian Culture

In his 'Navagraha Kirti', the great nineteenth-century Carnatic music composer Muthuswami Dikshitar describes Budh (the planet Mercury) as 'Napunsakam' or one who is not quite male or female. He alludes to a story in the Puranas where Brihaspati (the planet Jupiter) discovers that his wife Tara (the goddess of stars) is pregnant with the child of her lover, Chandra (the moon-god). He curses the love child to be born neither male nor female. The child is Budh. Budh later marries Ila, a man who becomes a woman when he accidentally trespasses into an enchanted grove. From that union springs the Chandra-vamsa, or the lunar dynasty of kings. So says the Mahabharata.

As in the story of Ila, Indian lore is full of tales where men turn into women and women turn into men. Narada falls into a pond, becomes a woman, discovers the meaning of worldly delusion or maya. Shiva bathes in the Yamuna, becomes a gopi or milkmaid, so that he can dance the raas-leela with Krishna—an idea that has inspired the temple of Gopeshwarji in Vrindavan. At a short distance from Ahmedabad is the temple of Bahucharji, the rooster-riding goddess, where it is said there was a pond that turned a woman into a man, a mare into a horse and a bitch into a dog. The pond has dried up, but women still visit this shrine seeking a male child. They seek the blessings of bhagats (some call them hijras) who, though men, believe they are women.

Near Pondicherry, in the village of Koovagam, every year the transgendered alis dance and sing in memory of an event that took place during mythic times. The son of Arjuna and his serpent wife, Ulupi, Aravan had to be sacrificed to ensure the victory of the Pandavas at Kurukshetra. But he refused to die without a taste of marriage. As no woman was willing to marry a man doomed to die the following dawn, Krishna took his female form, Mohini, and became Aravan's wife. Mohini spent a night with him and then wailed for him as his widow when Aravan was beheaded.

In the Valmiki Ramayana, there are descriptions of rakshasa women who kiss women on Ravana's bed on whose lips lingers the taste of their master. In the Krittivasa Ramayana is the story of two widows who drink a magic potion and, in the absence of their husband, make love to each other and end up bearing a child without bones (traditionally believed to be the contribution of semen).

How does one interpret these stories? Are they gay stories? They certainly shatter the conventional confines of gender and sexuality. Ancient Indian authors and poets without doubt imagined a state where the lines separating masculinity and femininity often blurred and even collapsed. Though awkward, these are not stray references. Such tales were consistent and recurring, narrated in a matter-of-fact way, without guilt or shame. Such outpouring has its roots in Indian metaphysics.

As the wheel of birth and rebirth turns, Indians have always believed, the soul keeps casting off old flesh and wrapping itself anew. Depending on one's karma, one can be reborn as a tree, as a rock, as a bird, a beast, a man, a woman, a man with a woman's heart, a woman with a man's heart, even as a god or demon ... endless possibilities exist in the infinite cosmos. The wise see masculinity and femininity as ephemeral robes that wrap the sexless, genderless soul. The point is not to get attached to the flesh but to celebrate its capabilities, discover its limitations, and finally transcend it.

The question before us is: does the human mind have the empathy to include gender and sexual ambiguity in civil human society? It does. In every yuga new rules come into being that redefine world order. The Mahabharata mentions a yuga when there was no marriage—women were free to go with any man they chose. This changed when Shvetaketu instituted the marriage laws. We have lived through a yuga where we left unchallenged the laws of old imperial masters that dehumanized and invalidated sexual minorities. Some laws have changed, but many hearts still resist.

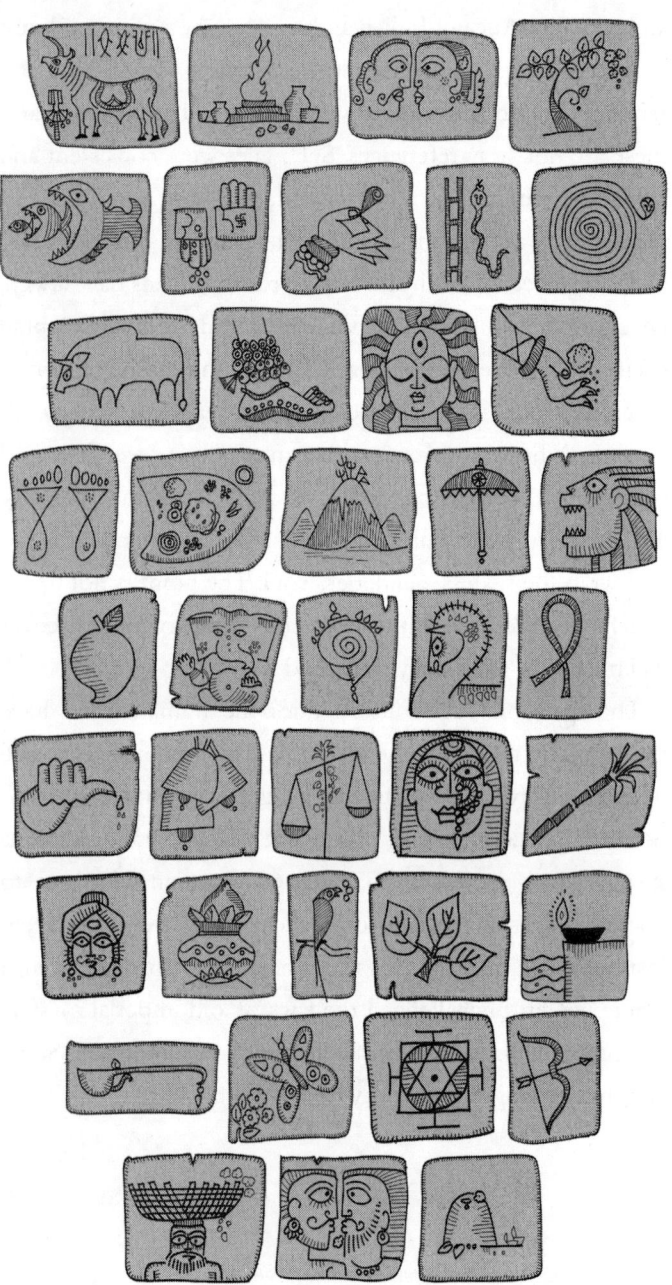

40

Moksha
Return to Samadhi

Many Hindus believe that a holy man does not die, but is able to voluntarily liberate, through yogic practices, his life-force (jiva-atma) from the mortal flesh (deha) so that it unites with the cosmic infinite life-force (param-atma).

As is commonly understood, samadhi refers to the tomb of a holy man, or a place where he is cremated. It could also be a place where his relics are stored. A famous example of a samadhi is Rajghat where Mahatma Gandhi's remains lie. Traditionally, most Hindus are cremated. However, a saint's dead body was buried, and the burial site became a holy shrine.

In the thirteenth century, the saint Dnyaneshwar wrote the first regional work on the Gita, called the *Dnyaneshwari*, in Marathi. We are told that he took samadhi at a very young age. The historian D.D. Kosambi referred to this step of his as ritual suicide. However, this annoyed many of Dnyaneshwar's devotees who refused to see samadhi as suicide. This could be because after the entrenchment of Christian mythology in modern thought suicide came to be seen as a 'sin against God'.

The idea of voluntarily killing oneself or setting one's jiva-atma free is part of Indian lore. At the end of the Ramayana, Sita enters the earth. After this Ram performs jal-samadhi by entering the waters of the Sarayu river. In Jainism the jiva-atma is set free through the practice of Sallekhana. This religious practice involves voluntarily fasting to death by gradually reducing the intake of food and liquids. We all know of the infamous and now illegal practice of sati, where women burnt themselves on the funeral pyre of their husbands.

But in the *Yoga Sutra*, the word samadhi is used at the final step of the eight-part yoga process (ashta-anga-yoga). And when gurus speak of it, they tend to be vague about what exactly it is. A clue lies perhaps in the logical progression seen from step 1 of the yoga sutra, which deals with relationships, to steps 2, 3, 4 and 5 which involve increased withdrawal from worldly life using self-discipline, body postures, breath manipulation and sensory control, to steps 6 and 7 which deal with mental exercises such as awareness and attention.

What would the logical eighth step be? Going further, deeper into the mind, and beyond, yes, but to realize what? The result we are told is kaivalya, or complete knowledge, of the whole universe. Patanjali equates this with a god-like state where we attain siddhi, with the power to walk on water and fly through the sky. Buddhism equates it with nothingness, or shunya. Hindus associate it with infinity, or ananta.

But could it be something simpler? The word samadhi is a fusion of two words: sama and adhi. Sama is the first beat of a musical cycle in Indian classical music, the return to the first note. Adhi means primal, or first. Thus, it can be interpreted as a return to the origin. What is our origin? What is the tree whose seed gave birth to our existence? Here, the answer may be two-fold.

In Vedanta, the tree is divinity, God, described variously as consciousness or super-consciousness, something that is non-material and hence outside the rules of space and time. In Tantra, the tree is the Goddess, nature itself. We discover our origins in nature, in matter, in hunger and fear. Vedanta gave rise to monastic traditions, which involve withdrawal of the senses, conquering hunger and fear. Tantra gave rise to sensual practices, often called occult, which basically involve amplification of the senses, feeling nourished and secure. Vedanta and Tantra are two branches of the Vedic tree.

Another way of looking at samadhi is to realize that it's the path that enables the monk (who has renounced the world) to return to the material world, at peace with the idea of death and suffering, master of his hunger and fear, sensitive to other people's hunger and fear. Some call it immortality. Some call it freedom from the fear of mortality (jiva-mukta). His entry into the tomb is actually a return (sama) to the source (adhi): the womb, as a hermit-householder (yogi-bhogi).

About the Author

Devdutt Pattanaik writes, illustrates and lectures on the relevance of mythology in modern times. He has, since 1996, written over fifty books and 1,000 columns on how stories, symbols and rituals construct the subjective truth (myths) of ancient and modern cultures around the world. To know more, visit devdutt.com.